Praise for *Countering M*

C000128256

"Alfred de Zayas is a precious res[...] in this wonderfully lucid collection of [...] time. With the wisdom of a seer and the knowledge of a world class jurist de Zayas is an authoritative voice of reason and equity in this precarious period of dangerous warmongering untruths. Don't weep, read and then act."

—RICHARD FALK, Former UN Special Rapporteur
and Professor Emeritus, Princeton University

"The ugliness of official lies and suppression of truth in our times is a serious threat to the possibility of a democratic society. Alfred de Zayas' book is a vigil for a society where press freedom means more than the freedom to buy the press and to lie without restraint."

—VIJAY PRASHAD, Professor of International Studies, Trinity College,
Executive-director of the Tricontinental Institute for Social Research

"Alfred de Zayas' *Countering Mainstream Narratives: Fake News, Fake Law, Fake Freedom* is a coherent and powerful pushback against manipulation by the media, which mirrors largely corporate hegemony, if not racist and xenophobic tendencies, which he meticulously and effectively documents.... De Zayas calls inter alia for a global commitment to the spiritual principles undergirding the UDHR, a Magna Carta for humanity, mirroring the values of major philosophical and belief systems. A must read for anyone wanting to create a socially just world constructed from a holistic vision of the interdependency and indivisibility of human rights, this book is truly a tour de force."

—DR. JOSEPH WRONKA, Professor, School of Social Work and
Behavioral Sciences, Springfield College, and Representative to the UN in
New York, International Association of Schools of Social Work

"A book every peace and human rights activist needs. The intrepid de Zayas beats new paths and, showing honest media as essential to democracy, he at the same time brilliantly illustrates how indispensable academic courage and freedom are to democracy."

—FREDRIK S. HEFFERMEHL, Norwegian jurist,
former vice-president of the International Peace Bureau (IPB),
founding member of the Lay Down Your Arms Association

"Alfred de Zayas empowers readers to consume the mainstream media 'wise as serpents' (Jesus Christ, Matthew 10:16) and to see through Fake News, Fake Law and Fake Freedom. This immaculately documented book is at the same time informative, philosophical, concise, clever and amusing."

—PROF. HARRO VON SENGER, Ph.D., D.J., Swiss jurist

"An honest book that appeals to reason in dealing with diplomacy, peace, and war. Erudite and endlessly quotable, even aphoristic, this book champions academic freedom and the right to seek and impart information."

—PROF. DR. ALEXANDRE LAMBERT, Geneva,
expert in multilateral organizations and international security

COUNTERING
MAINSTREAM NARRATIVES

FAKE NEWS • FAKE LAW • FAKE FREEDOM

ALFRED DE ZAYAS

Clarity Press, Inc.

© 2022 Alfred de Zayas

ISBN: 978-1-949762-66-2
EBOOK ISBN: 978-1-949762-67-9

In-house editor: Diana G. Collier
Book design: Becky Luening

ALL RIGHTS RESERVED: Except for purposes of review, this book may not be copied, or stored in any information retrieval system, in whole or in part, without permission in writing from the publishers.

Library of Congress Control Number: 2022939592

Clarity Press, Inc.
2625 Piedmont Rd. NE, Ste. 56
Atlanta, GA 30324, USA
https://www.claritypress.com

To all who strive for peace and freedom, whistleblowers like Julian Assange and Edward Snowden, who open our eyes to our gradual descent into Orwellian dystopia; to those who push back against mainstream indoctrination and brainwashing; to those who promote disarmament for development and human dignity

Table of Contents

THE INFORMATION WAR

THE WEAPONIZATION OF
HUMAN RIGHTS

DOUBLE STANDARDS

THE UKRAINE WAR:
CAUSES AND IMPLICATIONS

THE FUNCTIONS OF LAW

Preface

Like Julia and Winston in George Orwell's dystopian novel *1984,* we all live in a particular socio-economic environment that imposes a value system, influences the way we think, how we perceive the world around us, how we interrelate with others.

Human beings are social animals who want to belong. Accordingly, it is normal to go with the flow, to think inside the box, to evaluate facts and events in the light of a moral compass which has been suggested to us through education and group-think. We utilize those analytical tools we are familiar with and generally trust. Only a few lateral thinkers make an effort to test society's premises and venture to think outside the box, to look at things from different angles and perspectives.

Julia and Winston lived in a world of propaganda and indoctrination, manufactured consent, manufactured dissent, skewed narratives, cognitive dissonance, institutional intolerance and instinctive fear. While the world of 2022 is not that of Orwell's projections, doubtless there are parallels, compromising trends, peer pressure that merit our consideration if we want to avert chaos, avoid nuclear war, and survive as free agents capable to shape the world of 2050.

Some observers would claim that our ostensibly democratic governments have already equipped themselves with institutions that function like Oceania's Ministry of Truth, namely governmental "narrative management," press conferences, white papers and other pronouncements, frequently lacking sufficient substantiation and empirical evidence, which are dutifully und uncritically echoed by the mainstream media and compliant think tanks, which are often the source of same.

In the United States the Department of Homeland Security created in April 2022 a so-called Disinformation Narrative

Board,[1] headed by the controversial Nina Jankowicz, who has been critical of First Amendment Rights[2] on freedom of opinion and expression. Indeed, it appears that the U.S. government is more at war with dissent than with what it chooses to call "disinformation."

Meanwhile the U.S. is equipped with what could be seen as a branch office of Orwell's Ministry of Peace, which we like to call the Department of "Defense" (not the War Department, as it was called until 1949), which over the decades has engaged primarily in sabre-rattling and military aggression against other nations, entrusted to its executive arm, the North Atlantic Treaty Organization. As Orwell warned us: "Peace is War."

We have become accustomed to newspeak, doublethink, the thought police—what the Germans call "*Denkverbote*"— areas that our brains prophylactically tell us that it is better not to explore. Yet, our ubiquitous "political correctness" is a kind of soft power, not so scary, not too oppressive. It is more like *1984 Light*. Somehow it does not hurt. On the contrary, it even makes us feel more or less "safe."

We feel comfortable and comforted when we listen to empty rhetoric. We tend to trust our governments because we have been taught since grammar and high school that, of course, we are by definition the "good guys" and that our democracy is the best in the world. We do not readily see that imperial arrogance and narcissism masquerade as benevolent concern, that our sense of a "mission" drives us to aggress against other nations and deny

1 U.S. Department of Homeland Security, "Fact Sheet: DHS Internal Working Group Protects Free Speech and Other Fundamental Rights When Addressing Disinformation That Threatens the Security of the United States," May 2, 2022, https://www.dhs.gov/news/2022/05/02/fact-sheet-dhs-internal-working-group-protects-free-speech-other-fundamental-rights.

2 Stephen Dinan, "DHS created 'disinformation governance' team to track election misinformation," *The Washington Times,* April 28, 2022, https://www.washingtontimes.com/news/2022/apr/28/dhs-created-disinformation-governance-team-police-/; Lee Brown, "Disinformation czar Nina Jankowicz: Parents' anger at CRT 'weaponized' for profit," *New York Post,* May 5, 2022, https://nypost.com/2022/05/05/disinformation-czar-nina-jankowicz-crt-anger-being-weaponized/.

others the right to self-determination, to have their own set of values and beliefs. Only a few thinkers like Noam Chomsky have warned us that international law, humanitarian values and human rights have been quietly hijacked, instrumentalized for geopolitics, weaponized against the enemies of choice.

This collection of essays encompasses 26 pieces written for *Counterpunch* (including one essay together with Professor Richard Falk[3]) in 2021–22, enhanced by essays published in the UN staff magazine *New Special*[4] and by a draft encyclopaedia entry that had to be significantly watered down in order to pass the politically correct editors. The essays illustrate how far the information war has advanced, how a slick form of totalitarianism has become the "new normal," how dissenters are being "cancelled" by government and Bigtech, how our national budgets are squandered in the arms race, how the military-industrial complex—already condemned by Dwight Eisenhower in 1961[5]—is destroying what is left of our democracy.

The mainstream media—otherwise known as corporate media—plays a crucial role in destroying language, demonizing those who dare think independently and express their own opinions. Censorship and virtual book-burnings are widespread, while the growing pressure of conformism leads many to self-censorship—or career death. Yet, we cannot yet speak of the globalization of fear, because very few people feel genuinely menaced by our own governments or by the dictates of peer pressure. As long as we continue getting our daily dose of *panem et circensis*,[6] we actually kind of like our "Big Brother."

---

3 Alfred de Zayas and Richard Falk, Reflections on Genocide as the Ultimate Crime." *CounterPunch,* April 23, 2021, https://www.counterpunch.org/author/alfred-de-zayas-richard-falk/.

4 *newSpecial,* https://www.newspecial.org.

5 "Eisenhower's Warning about the Military-Industrial Complex" [1961], YouTube video posted July 20, 2020 by Bernie Sanders, 1:54, https://www.youtube.com/watch?v=SEGpTu8sVKI.

6 "bread and circuses"—from Roman poet Juvenal's *Satire X (Satura X),* ca. 120 CE, line 81.

Modern-day "hate weeks,"[7] similar to those conducted against the designated enemies of Oceania in Orwell's novel, direct our hostility not only against the leaders of other countries, including Belarus, Bolivia, China, Cuba, Iran, Russia, Syria, Venezuela, but also against the culture and literature of these countries, and ultimately against their hapless population, because our media suggests guilt by association. We condemn the Russian population because of their refusal to rebel against their leaders and embrace our neo-liberal and geopolitical worldview. We cancel the Russian soprano Anna Netrebko[8] and the Russian conductor Valery Gergiev,[9] we cancel Tchaikovsky[10] and Dostoyevsky.[11]

Similarly, we want to perceive not only the Russians but also the Chinese as "enemies," because they do not immediately follow our leadership, refuse to align their economies with ours and decline to disavow their leaders—as if that were an easy task.

The mantra "You are either with us or against us"[12] is being forced on many people. Predictably, this totalitarian mindset

---

7 In Orwell's novel, "hate week" is an operation conducted by Oceania's government aimed at magnifying the fears and increasing the hatred that the population feels. It is directed at the two opposing superstates Eurasia and Eastasia, as well as at the mythical leader of the "Brotherhood" (see "Hate Week," *Book Analysis,* https://bookanalysis.com/1984/hate-week/). During hate week there are parades, speeches, lectures, new slogans are coined, new songs put out.

8 Samantha Ibrahim, "Anna Netrebko, Russian soprano with ties to Putin, out at Metropolitan Opera," *New York Post,* March 4, 2022, https://nypost.com/2022/03/04/russian-soprano-anna-netrebko-out-at-met-opera-over-putin-support/.

9 Nick Vivarelli, "Russian Conductor Who Supports Putin Dropped by Carnegie Hall and Faces Exit From Milan's La Scala Following Ukraine Invasion," *Variety,* February 25, 2022, https://variety.com/2022/music/news/valery-gergiev-la-scala-carnegie-hall-1235190084/#!

10 Billy Binion, "Tchaikovsky Is Canceled," *Reason,* March 9, 2022, https://reason.com/2022/03/09/cardiff-philharmonic-orchestra-tchaikovsky-is-canceled/.

11 Chloe Stillwell, "A university tried to ban Dostoevsky to ... punish Putin?" *MIC,* March 2, 2022, https://www.mic.com/culture/dostoevsky-banned-russia-ukraine.

12 "'You are either with us or against us,'" *CNN.com,* November 6, 2001, https://edition.cnn.com/2001/US/11/06/gen.attack.on.terror/

and the accompanying institutionalized intransigence heighten tensions, provoke push-back, and generate negative results, because no one likes to be blackmailed.

Patriotism is reduced to the formula "my country right or wrong"—instead of representing a commitment to do our level best to create the conditions for social justice at home and peace and stability internationally. True patriots demand from government and civil society a genuine commitment to peace, international law and the UN Charter. True patriots understand the dangers of nuclear escalation and propose disarmament for development. True patriots demand transparency and accountability from our leaders. True patriots reject the unconstitutional surveillance conducted by the CIA and National Security Agency.[13]

Notwithstanding the above considerations, there is room for a measure of optimism, because we can still seek and obtain the information we need in order to develop our own judgment over facts and events. We can fact-check what we read in the "quality press," we can still compare and discuss different interpretations with our friends and acquaintances. Indeed, there are plenty of experts, professors of international law, international relations, history, sociology, psychology, and many journalists who do think independently and refuse to follow the prescribed "narrative." There are independent, alert thinkers who have managed to retain a sense for objectivity and a faculty of self-criticism.

It is still possible to write coherent analyses of events and stay clear of political manipulation and propaganda. I can think of many reliable sources and balanced analyses, including those by Professor John Mearsheimer in Chicago, Prof. Jeffrey Sachs in New York, Prof. Richard Falk in Santa Barbara, Prof. Francis Boyle in Illinois, Prof. Dan Kovalik in Pittsburgh, Prof. Stephen Kinzer in Boston, Prof. Marjorie Cohn in San Diego, Prof. Nils Melzer in Geneva, Prof. Harro von Senger in Lausanne, Prof. Reinhard Merkel in Hamburg, Professor Axel Schoenberger in

---

13 National Security Agency/Central Security Service, https://www.nsa.gov/.

Bremen, Professor Karl Albrecht Schachtschneider in Erlangen, Curtis Doebbler in Washington DC, Marc Weisbrot in Washington DC, Alyn Ware in New Zealand, Glenn Greenwald[14] in Rio de Janeiro, Max Blumenthal of The Grayzone, Aaron Maté of Pushback, Lindsay German in London, the British journalist Adriel Kasonta in London, the Scottish journalist Alan MacLeod in Edinburgh, the Australian Caitlin Johnstone in Melbourne, etc. On the conservative side there are also many challenging voices, including those of Patrick Buchanan,[15] Scott Horton,[16] Keith Knight,[17] Rand Paul,[18] Paul Craig Roberts,[19] and Ron Paul.[20]

Moreover, the internet is full of pertinent information and analyses that do not peddle the doctrinal agenda of the mainstream media. Anyone who wants to understand what is going

---

14 Shaye Galletta, "Glenn Greenwald on Russia-Ukraine: What about border dispute justifies US risking annihilation of the planet?" *Fox News,* April 27, 2022, https://www.foxnews.com/media/glenn-greenwald-on-russia-ukraine-tucker-carlson-today-fox-nation.

15 Patrick J. Buchanan, "Understanding the Ukraine/Russia War – Pat Buchanan," *Boston Broadside,* February 25, 2022, https://www.bostonbroadside.com/national/understanding-the-ukraine-russia-war-pat-buchanan/.

16 Scott Horton, "The History Behind the Russia-Ukraine War," March 3, 2022, *Antiwar.com,* https://original.antiwar.com/scott/2022/03/02/the-history-behind-the-russia-ukraine-war/

17 Keith Knight, "SHOCKING: Pat Buchanan Predicts NATO Expansion to Cause Russia/Ukraine/US War in 1999," *Don't Tread on Anyone* podcast, https://podcasts.apple.com/us/podcast/shocking-pat-buchanan-predicts-nato-expansion-to-cause/id1542461279?i=1000552262734; Keith Knight, "NATO Countries Arm Ukraine: What the Corporate Press REFUSES to Say About Russia and The Donbas War," *The Libertarian Institute,* March 12, 2022, https://libertarianinstitute.org/dont-tread-on-anyone/nato-125/.

18 Kylie Atwood and Jennifer Hansler, "Rand Paul argues US should not have backed Ukraine's NATO aspirations, citing Russia's stated reasoning behind invasio," *CNN,* April 27, 2022, https://edition.cnn.com/2022/04/26/politics/rand-paul-russia-ukraine-comments/index.html.

19 "The function of the Western media is to turn fiction into fact and lie into truth. Once the narrative is established, it is repeated endlessly." Paul Craig Roberts, "Ukraine Update #2," *Institute for Political Economy,* February 25, 2022, https://www.paulcraigroberts.org/2022/02/25/ukraine-update-2/.

20 Ron Paul, "The Ukraine War Is a Racket," *CNS News,* April 25, 2022, https://cnsnews.com/commentary/ron-paul/ron-paul-ukraine-war-racket.

on should proactively seek the information on the internet and elsewhere, discuss it with friends and family. It is no longer possible to rely only on the "quality press." that has shown itself to be in the service of the establishment, and often enough, in the service of the military-industrial-financial complex.

Personally, I have always been an advocate of greater space for civil society initiatives and have been a grass-roots activist and member of several non-governmental organizations. While I salute NGOs and their members for their courageous work in making human rights visible and in promoting good causes, I must also acknowledge that over the years the human-rights movement has been penetrated by corporations, special interests, lobbies, intelligence services and other operatives who do not have human dignity as their principal concern. Indeed, some NGOs have made a lucrative business out of human rights and some are very happy to work with Big Brother.

Gradually we understand that the principal target of Big Brother is not "the enemy" of the day, the Russians or the Chinese, the geoeconomic rival or competitor—but us. A contemporary "Room 101" awaits those who do not bend to the invitation of political correctness. Cancel culture has become socially acceptable, and some in the social media are even more incendiary than our political leaders. We are gradually becoming the principal target of the globalization of a kind of metaphysical terror.

In the end, we cannot escape the conclusion that our control institutions have betrayed us, that we cannot rely on the "rule of law." due process, the "presumption of innocence," the right to access information, the right to truth, the right of freedom of opinion, not even the right to freedom of religion and conviction. The gradual politicization of law has corrupted the system of the administration of civil and criminal justice into a political battlefield, in which law is a weapon of war, what we know as "lawfare."

We observe that domestic and international courts have been corrupted. Even the human rights tribunals have been penetrated by corporate interests, intelligence services, our all-knowing Big Brother. *Quis custodiet ipsos custodes?* (Juvenalis, *Satires, VI, 347–48*). Who will guard over the guardians? Only ourselves. We have little choice. We simply must be the guardians of our own fate. Orwell gave us a wake-up call and we slept right through it. Whistle-blowers like Julian Assange and Edward Snowden gave us repeated warnings, and we have failed time and again to take the necessary steps to protect ourselves and succeeding generations. We must act now. Our future is in our hands.

—Afred de Zayas, Geneva, June 2022

Acknowledgments

Although this is not a treatise in international law, I have benefited from the wisdom of many international lawyers with whom I am in regular contact, and whose books I have read, including Professors Noam Chomsky, Richard Falk, John Mearsheimer, Jeffrey Sachs, Stephen Kinzer, Francis Boyle, Dan Kovalik, Karl Albrecht Schachtschneider, as well as my peers at the Genena School of Diplomacy, and many students, from whom I have drawn fresh ideas. As Seneca put it—*docendo discimus*—we learn while teaching—and we learn from our students.

I am also indebted to the Geneva International Peace Research Institute, where I have received insights that are reflected in several of my essays. I must especially express my gratitude to my editor Diana Collier, a jewel in today's difficult publishing landscape.

Acknowledgments

THE
INFORMATION
WAR

1.

The *J'Accuse* of Our Time: The Persecution of Julian Assange

It may appear unnecessary to repeat the truism that democracy depends on transparency and accountability, and yet, how often has the democratic order been betrayed by our leaders in the recent past? How often have the media abandoned their watchdog function, how often have they simply accepted to provide an echo-chamber for the powerful, whether government or transnational corporations?

Among the many scandals and betrayals of democracy and the rule of law we recognize the persecution of inconvenient journalists by governments and their helpers in non-governmental organizations and the corporate media.

Perhaps the most immoral example of the multinational corruption of the rule of law is the scandalous "lawfare" campaign conducted against Julian Assange, the founder of Wikileaks, who in the year 2010 published evidence of war crimes and crimes against humanity committed by the United States and its NATO allies in Afghanistan and Iraq, provided to him by Chelsey Manning, an American intelligence officer and a wizard with computers.

In a world where the rule of law matters, these war crimes would have been promptly investigated, indictments would have been issued in the countries concerned. But no, the ire of the governments and the media focused instead on the journalist who had dared to uncover these crimes. The persecution of this journalist was a coordinated assault on the rule of law by the United States, United Kingdom and Sweden, later joined by Ecuador.

The instrumentalization of the administration of justice—not for purposes of doing justice, but to destroy a human being went on to pull more and more people into this joint criminal conspiracy of defamation, trumped-up charges, investigations without indictments, deliberate delays and coverups.

In April 2021 my colleague, Professor Nils Melzer, the UN Rapporteur on torture, published a meticulously researched and methodically unassailable documentation of this almost incredible saga, *Der Fall Julian Assange* (Piper Verlag, Munich) translated by Professor Melzer into English and published in February 2022 by Verso Press, New York, under the title *The Trial of Julian Assange*. This monumental indictment can well be called the *"J'accuse"* of our time, protesting and documenting how our authorities have betrayed us, how four governments colluded in the corruption of the rule of law.

Like Emile Zola, who in 1898 exposed the web of lies surrounding the scandalous judicial framing of the French Colonel Alfred Dreyfus in France, Nils Melzer shocks us 122 years later with proof of how countries that are ostensibly committed to the rule of law and human rights can betray that democratic ethos and be aided in doing so by the complicity of the mainstream media. Melzer provides "concrete evidence of political persecution, gross arbitrariness on the part of the administration of justice and deliberate torture and abuse."

This is an enormously important book because it requires us to abandon our "comfort zone" and demand transparency and accountability from our governments. Indeed, it is scandalous that none of the four governments involved in the frame-up cooperated with Professor Melzer, a UN Rapporteur, after all, and only answered with "political platitudes." I, too, as a UN Independent Expert on International Order, experienced a similar lack of cooperation from powerful countries to whom I addressed numerous *notes verbales* concerning violations of human rights. None of them responded satisfactorily.

Melzer reminds us of the Hans-Christian Andersen fable, "The Emperor's new clothes." Indeed, everyone involved in the Assange frame-up consistently maintains the illusion of legality and repeats the same untruths, until an astute observer says—*But the emperor has no clothes*! That is the point. Our administration of justice has no clothes and instead of advancing justice, it has colluded in the persecution of a journalist, with all the implications that this behavior has for the survival of the democratic order and freedom of the press.

Melzer's litany of facts clearly demonstrates that we are living in a time of "post-truth." It is our responsibility to correct this situation now, lest we wake up in a tyranny.

2.

Fake News, Fake History, Fake Law

"Fake news" is a widespread phenomenon—not only in wartime, but also in daily political and economic relations. Fake news items are not only disseminated by governments and its proxies, but also practiced by the private sector, by media conglomerates, by individuals in their correspondence, gossip, social media and through the internet.

Fake news is as prevalent in Europe as it is in the United States, in Latin America, Africa and Asia. Patently false narratives, false flag operations and bogus incidents are concocted by governments in order to justify their policies, enabled by a compliant corporate media acting as echo chambers of the propaganda they issue. Purportedly independent journalists (with their own agendas) have no hesitation to print evidence-free allegations, referring to anonymous officials or witnesses, supported by "secret intelligence." Thus emerges "fragmented truth," to the point that no one really knows what truth is; everyone clings to his own views, while refusing to consider alternative versions of the facts. When it comes to access to reliable information, freedom of opinion and expression, we live in an increasingly polarized, intolerant, intransigent world.

Only reluctantly we must acknowledge that "fake news" has always been around, the difference being that in the past only governments were purveyors of fake news, only governments could successfully manipulate public opinion, whereas today anybody with access to the internet can also weigh in. From experience we also know that all media—CNN, CBC, BBC, DW, *New York Times*, *Washington Post*, *The Times*, *The Economist*, *Le Monde*, *Le Figaro*, the *Frankfurter Allgemeine Zeitung*, the *Neue Zürcher Zeitung*, *El Pais*, *El Mundo*, RT, Sputnik, CGTN, Global Times, Xinhua, Asia Times, Telesur,

Prensa Latina—all slant the news in a particular way. They cite their favorite pundits and distort the facts, whether by lying here and there, suppressing inconvenient facts and opinions, or shamelessly applying double-standards.

The perception of contemporary events eventually generates "fake history," which necessarily builds on the steady flow of both verifiable information and fake news. As an aspiring historian taking courses in the Harvard Graduate School of Arts and Sciences (at the same time as I was getting my law degree), as a doctoral candidate in history at the Philosophical Faculty of the University of Göttingen in Germany, I learned to question historical narratives, look at the sources, insist on seven Cs of history writing; chronology, context, coherence, comprehensiveness, causality, comparison and *cui bono* (who stands to gain from an event and from a particular interpretation). I was taught never to rely on a single source, but proactively to look for alternative views, see whether the standard narrative can be challenged, whether there has been a subsequent publication of previously classified documents, whether the memoirs of movers and shakers, politicians and diplomats suggest the necessity of adjusting the mainstream narrative.

My research activities for my publications on the Spanish Civil War and on the Second World War and its aftermath convinced me that history textbooks were not all that reliable, that some of them were essentially propagating oversimplifications that ignored crucial facts, that long debunked canards had found their way into the mainstream narrative, sometimes resulting in a caricature of events. Given my ability to read the original documents in English, French, German, Spanish, Dutch and Russian, my research in public and private archives in the U.S., Canada, United Kingdom, France, Germany, the Netherlands, Switzerland, and Spain opened my horizons far beyond the accepted narratives. On the other hand, I also realized that archives could be incomplete, that inconvenient documents could have been destroyed, that pertinent information could still be classified and thus inaccessible.

Personal interviews with key players like George F. Kennan, Robert Murphy, James Riddleberger, Telford Taylor, Benjamin Ferencz, Howard Levie, Lord Strang, Lord Paget, Lord Weidenfeld, Lord Thomas, Sir Geoffrey Harrison, Sir Denis Allen, Albert Speer, Karl Dönitz, Otto Skorzeny, General Friedrich Hossbach, Otto von Habsburg, Kurt Waldheim, added missing links and nuances. I was able to connect the dots.

I also realized that the optimistic expectation that as time passes and emotions abate, the historical narrative will become more objective is a sorry illusion. Frequently the very opposite happens, because as the persons in the know disappear, as witnesses die and no one is left to dispute the politically useful narrative, pseudo-history is cemented and emerges as the socially accepted narrative. Extrapolating from my experience researching 20th century historical events, I am convinced that our knowledge of Mesopotamian, Egyptian, Greek and Roman times, our perception of the Middle Ages, the Renaissance, the Napoleonic era, must be woefully incomplete. I also realize that it will be very difficult to change the established narratives—absent some extraordinary discovery of previously unknown manuscripts of diplomatic or commercial correspondence, papyrus or cuneiform tablets.

What also amazes me is that no one seems to be talking about "fake law." Indeed, politicians and journalists frequently "invent" law as they go along, contending that what some lobby or interest group invokes as law actually has legal force, as if law and legal obligations could spontaneously arise, without the drafting, negotiation and adoption process of all legislation, treaties, conventions, or without the ratification by parliaments.

We must beware of the loose use of legal terms, which undermines the authority and credibility of the law. Not every military encounter entails "aggression," not every massacre constitutes "genocide," not every form of sexual harassment can be

considered "rape." Nor is every jailed politician a "political prisoner," nor every migrant a "refugee." And yet, much hyperbole
and political agitation play out on this pseudo-legal arena, much
political blackmail is practiced on the basis of fake "law," and
so much of what is actually simply propaganda is believed by
average citizens. But then, *mundus vult decipi* (the world wants
to be deceived).

Politicians who want to impose sanctions insist that they are
legal, without, however, elucidating the legal basis or feeling the
need to. In classical international law unilateral coercive measures are not legal. The only legal sanctions are those imposed
by the UN Security Council under article VII of the Charter. All
other unilateral coercive measures actually constitute an illegal
"use of force," prohibited in article 2(4) of the Charter, and contrary to article 2(3), which requires negotiations in good faith.

Moreover, the extra-territorial application of national law
(e.g. the U.S.'s Helms-Burton Act) violates numerous principles
of the United Nations, including the sovereign equality of states,
the self-determination of peoples, freedom of commerce and
freedom of navigation.

Daily, governments and the media invent their own law—
but it is bogus law. Alas, the media simply disseminates this
"fake law," which then is interwoven with "fake news"—and
people believe it.

Some politicians pretend that there is a human right to
migration but fail to give any treaty or doctrinal source. Of
course, every sovereign state can generously open its borders
and welcome both economic migrants and refugees, but this
opening of frontiers is nowhere required by international law.
True enough, the 1951 Geneva Refugee Convention requires
states parties to give refugee status to individuals who enter their
territory and can substantiate a risk of persecution for purposes
of the Convention, but this entails individual refugee status
determination and does not invite uncontrolled massive refugee
entry. The very ontology of a sovereign state since the Peace

of Westphalia is that the state controls its frontiers and deter-
mines who can and cannot enter its territory.[21] This is customary
international law recognized in every textbook.

There is, of course, the UN Convention on the Rights
of Migrant Workers and Members of their Families, but this
Convention applies only to migrant workers who have already
entered the territory and have their papers in order. Moreover,
the Convention does not establish a right of migration, it only
specifies the rights of migrant workers living within the State's
jurisdiction. It should also be noted that only 56 countries have
ratified the MWC—the U.S., Canada, UK, France, Germany,
Italy, Belgium, Netherlands, Norway, Sweden, Denmark, and
Spain are among those which have not.

All too often we are confronted by a combination of fake
news, fake history and fake law, a very toxic cocktail for any
democracy. Alas, fake law has become a favorite weapon of
demagogues and phoney "experts" and "diplomats" who glee-
fully engage in what might as well be termed "fake diplomacy,"
as their goal is not to reach a reasonable negotiated settlement,
but rather to score points on the gladiator arena of power-politics,
with the dutiful collusion of a sold-out and capricious media.

The unsuccessful encounters between Putin and Biden,
between Lavrov and Blinken belong in this category of "fake
diplomacy." Indeed, unless we do away with fake news, fake
history and fake law, it will be very difficult to advance true
diplomacy in the sense of George F. Kennan. Thus continues the
game of sabre-rattling and sanctions that have brought the world
to a situation of armed conflict, which could even degenerate
into World War III. In the process many fortunes are being made,
since nothing is more lucrative than the arms business, and the
military-industrial-financial complex has an economic interest
in stoking tensions and prolonging war.

---

21 Karl Doehring, "Aliens, Admission," in R. Bernhardt, *Encyclopaedia of
Public International Law* (Amsterdam: North Holland Publishing Co., 1992), I:107–
109; also Doehring, "Aliens, Expulsion and Deportation," in Bernhardt: 109–112.

Is there a solution to "fake news"? Demagogues would establish an Orwellian "Ministry of Truth." others would criminalize "fake news" (but only inconvenient "fake news"), others would pretend to filter facts and opinion using self-made tools to determine what is true and what isn't.

No one needs this kind of Inquisition and censorship, because neither governments nor the private sector can be gate-keepers of the truth. The only solution is to ensure pluralistic access to information and global open debate. Society must demand greater transparency at all levels and be enabled to proactively seek the truth by consulting multiple sources and making a new synthesis, which will not be "revealed truth" or "immutable truth." but a constantly evolving truth that incorporates the complexity and nuances of reality on the ground.

All of the above raises the question whether we are not already living under a fake democracy? What kind of correlation is there between the will and needs of the people and the laws and regulations that govern them? Is there not a great disconnect between governments and the people? Are there any democratic governments where the people actually can fully take part in the conduct of public affairs as envisaged in article 25 of the International Covenant on Civil and Political Rights? Where is the power of initiative and the right to hold referendums recognized? Surely the meaning of democracy must encompass more than the ritual act of going to the polls once every two or four years. Surely the democratic process must allow public input on real policy choices, not just pro-forma voting for one of two candidates.

In my reports to the General Assembly and Human Rights Council I insisted that those individuals who are elected do not really govern, while those who govern are not elected. I deplored the fact that "representative democracy" can only be called democratic if the Parliamentarians actually represent the views and wishes of the electorate, if they proactively inform the electorate and proactively consult with them. As an American I have noted that U.S. elections do not permit real choices, and that we can only exercise the fake right to vote for A or B, knowing that both A and B are committed to the military-industrial complex, that both support Wall Street over Main Street, that both are for capitalism with no caveats, and in foreign affairs both are hawks, both are interventionists, both prefer to engage in military interventions than to negotiate in good faith.

This ontological disconnect made me conclude that the two-party system we know in the United States cannot be regarded as much more democratic than the one-party system that rules China.

Democracy means rule by and for the people. Alas, we do not enjoy democracy and must content ourselves with the window-dressing, with the pro-forma rhetoric, with the trappings of democracy.

It is time for the American people to demonstrate the courage to demand an end to fake news, fake history, fake law, fake diplomacy, and fake democracy. But to achieve that we must first win the information war and defeat those who systematically brainwash the public. It will take time to reform the system, but this is a task we cannot avoid. We owe it to future generations. If there are to be any.

3.

How to Cope with the Deep State

Persons moderately informed have a vague idea of what the "deep state" means. Of course, we do not see the "deep state," but only evidence of its impacts. We discern contours through the actions of its agents—imbalances, arbitrariness, dislocations, extrapolations, logical leaps.

One cannot rely entirely on deductive reasoning (top-down logic) or inductive logic (bottom-up), because in a world of governmental secrecy, "fake news" and "fake law," our very premises are uncertain. We can try inductive reasoning and base ourselves on our own observations and other empirical data, but we must acknowledge that our sample is woefully incomplete.

Some persons tend to dismiss narratives about the "deep state" as a kind of "conspiracy theory." Out of sight, out of mind. We perceive the day-to-day functioning of our institutions as a normal routine operation, more or less following the "laws" of the marketplace or the anonymous forces of nature, not visualizing the extent to which the deep state can influence and manage these forces. What is the "deep state," then? We can recognize it on the faces of our corporate elite in their fancy boardrooms. But not only there.

Closer to our skins is our social environment, the pervasive *Zeitgeist* created by the daily indoctrination by the corporate media, television, movies, even comic-books, which ably combine actual "fake news" with the suppression of crucial facts, advancing the subliminal message that we are "the good guys" and that our governments' actions are not only "legal" but also legitimate, noble and honorable.

Our media engages in what some may consider "benevolent brainwashing," but in fact, it is well-calculated hot-and-cold onslaughts, sometimes "fear mongering" against foreign "enemies," horror stories about natural disasters and pandemics, speculation over their origins—alternating with the dissemination of trivial "feel good" stories. As long as most of the population gets *panem et circensis* (Juvenalis), we will pose no danger to the deep state.

The result of the constant indoctrination is that public opinion is homologated.

Independent thinkers are made to feel isolated, and the phenomenon of self-censorship gradually sets in, because most people want to "belong" to a "majority." Groupthink is safe. Only a few dare to be odd man out. Thus, whether willingly or unwillingly, we tend to accept the lies that are fed to us by the media—because it is the easiest way to deal with the monstrosities that our governments are perpetrating throughout the world. The world *wants* to be deceived.

The "deep state" ably creates unreality, manages our perception of facts and context through a compliant corporate media. It operates through an unholy alliance consisting of the media, intelligence services, generalized surveillance and private sector censorship through Big Tech. You might call it an axis of evil, dressed up as "democratic governance."

There is an incestuous relationship between the deep state and the think tanks and opportunistic academics, "pens for hire," who produce deep-state-friendly scenarios for us to consume. These think tanks are powerful lobby groups that are funded by interested parties, whether states, billionaires or military. It is ironic that we are actually paying for our own indoctrination, since our tax dollars are used to finance the whole apparatus, research and development into more effective tools of control, generalized surveillance of our every move.

Is there an escape from the "deep state" and its many scams? Will voting Democratic or Republican get us out of it? No, because both parties serve the deep state—the corporations and the military-industrial-financial complex.

Does this situation remind us of the ending of Orwell's *1984*? How Winston was psychologically broken by the horror of the rats in room 101, and he even abandoned his only love, Julia, denouncing her so that she be tortured instead of him? Yes, Winston is released from the Ministry of Love and now leads a meaningless dehumanized life. When once he encounters Julia again, she admits that she too had betrayed him. Their human relationship, their values were extinguished. Orwell's novel closes with Winston looking at an image of Big Brother. There he experiences a curious sense of victory, because now he loves Big Brother.

What can we do? Surrender? No. We have not reached this point. While we still can, we must demand transparency and accountability from our elected officials. There are plenty of good people out there. Not all politicians and journalists are consciously part of the "deep state"—they are individuals like us, caught in the well-oiled machinery.

We must resolutely push back against the lies of the corporate media, against the tyranny of political correctness and the conformism of our peers. We must use the democratic tools at our disposal and exercise our civil rights at the municipal and local level first, before we can tackle challenges at the federal and international levels. We must pro-actively seek and impart information on all issues, educate our children and our friends. We must demand from our governments respect for the existing and actual "rules-based international order"—the UN Charter, not as touted by U.S. officials in support of their policies which contradict it. We must demand true democracy, regular consultations, genuine choices, participation in the conduct of public affairs, referenda, people power. Pushback against Orwellian newspeak and the ongoing destruction of language. We must refuse to retreat into self-censorship.

4.

Facts Without Consequences

"Fake news" and "post-truth" are popular neologisms—but they have actually been part of the political landscape for a very long time. We have learned to live with fake news, fake history and bogus law. We swim in an ocean of lies and disinformation, but somehow manage to survive the economic and political sharks all around us.

What is far more worrisome is the actuality that there are "real facts" that cry out for our attention, that demand urgent action, and that our politicians and media treat as non-existent or marginal concerns, e.g. exorbitant military expenses, skewed national budgets, xenophobic war-mongering, structural violence, military aggression, unilateral coercive measures, financial blockades, media homologation, manifestly unjust laws, the corruption of the "rule of law" through legal scams and "lawfare," the penetration of public institutions by intelligence services, the "weaponization" of human rights, the imprisonment of whistle-blowers like Julian Assange, unjust taxation, tax havens, tax evasion, corporate bribery, economic exploitation, ecocide, extreme poverty, man-made famine, social exclusion, etc.

Now pause, take a breath and ask yourself why these facts are largely ignored or trivialized by politicians and media alike. Why are these "inconvenient" facts shoved aside, as if they were only of marginal importance or as if they did not exist? Without a doubt these facts engender short-term, medium-term and long-term consequences, create or perpetuate imbalances and spread a vague, destabilizing sense of incoherence and cognitive dissonance.

"Facts without consequences" constitute a *sui generis* category of reality. The facts may be public and easily available on the internet. But although they may be generally acknowledged—this happens under the condition that no genuine debate will be conducted concerning their veracity or urgency and that no concrete action will be taken to address them. It is worse than a conspiracy of silence. It constitutes a revolt against cognitive consistency, a betrayal of our responsibility to ourselves and others to be truthful and predictable, to draw the logical consequences and act thereon.

There are also "books without consequences." books without the urgent, imperative follow-up. Whereas some trash books like Francis Fukuyama's *The End of History and the Last Man* are given enormous attention, hugely relevant and challenging books by Noam Chomsky, John Mearsheimer, Richard Falk, Stephen Kinzer, William Blum, Jeffrey Sachs, Norman Finkelstein, Jacques Baud, Nils Melzer, Edward Snowden, and President Jimmy Carter are published by notable houses, but there is no follow-up.

One would have expected that after the publication of Chomsky's *Necessary Illusions: Thought Control in Democratic Societies*, Kinzer's *Overthrow*, Sachs' *The End of Poverty*, Melzer's *The Trial of Julian Assange*, Baud's *Gouverner par le Fake News*, Snowden's *Permanent Record*, David Stannard's *American Holocaust*, Norman Finkelstein's *Gaza*, Carter's *Our Endangered Values*, or Mearsheimer's *The Great Delusion*, scholarly conferences would have followed, triggering a genuine democratic discussion in townhalls, in the daily press, in the internet, throughout the spectrum of the media. Politically, these and other necessary books were intellectual dynamite, milestones in political thought. And precisely because of that these books were met mostly by silence, by a refusal to come to grips with the issues raised. These books had and still have the potential to advance international law and human rights. The establishment, however, avoids them like the devil avoids holy water. This explains why these books are victims of "benign neglect."

The facts are there and can be consulted in official documents and on the internet. The books are there and can be fact-
checked. We know that grave crimes have been committed and
are being committed by our governments. We should be able to
shout, "*Not in our name!*" but those who do so are often mobbed
or ridiculed, while the corporate media ignores both the issues
and the protests. We know that the United States government
has overthrown government after government throughout Latin
America and the world, that the CIA has destabilized countries
in Europe and the Middle East and financed coups d'état. We
know what Assange and Snowden have revealed, but there is
a tacit agreement in the media not to pursue these facts, but to
distract us with the demonization of our geopolitical rivals and
with other more "convenient" facts.

When important facts and publications are deliberately kept
out of the political narrative, the core of democracy is being
undermined. We observe this in the totally skewed narrative in
the Western media concerning the current war in Ukraine. Such
manipulation of public opinion is hugely dangerous, because the
disinformation and suppression of genuine debate may lead us
straight into World War III and nuclear apocalypse. President
Carter was not exaggerating when he said that the U.S. is "the
most warlike nation in the history of the world."[22]

This abnormal state of affairs quite naturally generates
"conspiracy theories," because, as Spinoza wrote in his *Ethics*,
"nature abhors a vacuum." If people are deprived of the truth,
if they cannot access information, they quite naturally start formulating hypotheses. No wonder that when the elites ignore or
suppress facts, the vacuum is often filled by wild speculation.

The governmental and media selective indignation and
application of the law *à la carte* predictably subverts the system
of governance and makes societies lose faith in the rule of law,

---

22 Simon Osborne, "Former President Carter brands US 'most WARLIKE"
nation on earth," *Express*, April 16, 2019, https://www.express.co.uk/news/
world/1115145/former-us-president-jimmy-carter-china-donald-trump.

or at least in their leadership and institutions. The attempt to deal with "fake news" through censorship and "hate speech" legislation is futile as it will only drive discussions underground and provoke an atmosphere of terror and fear, as our societies move closer and closer to the totalitarianism that Orwell anticipated and tried to avert.

What is needed is easier access to all pertinent information and pluralistic views, more open debate—not less! The internet must remain free of political controls—whether by government or the private sector. Official censorship of RT and Sputnik, private-sector censorship by Twitter, Facebook, and YouTube constitute a frontal attack on everyone's right to know, everyone's right to access to information as stipulated in article 19 of the International Covenant on Civil and Political Rights. Everyone should be able to arrive at his or her own judgment. Only thus can societies meaningfully exercise democratic rights and responsibilities. Censorship constitutes an assault on democracy.

There must not be "filters" to test the truth of digital exchanges. The only legitimate controls are those to suppress pornography, warmongering, incitement to hatred and violence, racketeering and other scams. In democratic societies no filters should be imposed in order to suppress the dissemination of factual information that the mainstream media deliberately ignores, nor to suppress an alternative interpretation of facts and events. What we need is a "culture of civilized dissent"—where everyone can express his/her opinions without the threat of career death and social ostracism. We need to reaffirm the *right to be wrong*—because only by preserving the possibility to err do we remain independent. Artistic, scientific, sociological progress depends on the freedom to postulate hypotheses, different models, different perspectives—which sometimes will be correct and sometimes not. A failed hypothesis should not be criminalized; rather, its fallacies should be exposed. The alternative is stagnation in homologation, robotization, Orwellian dystopia. The conformism of the current *Zeitgeist* is unworthy of democratic societies. It is up to us to vindicate the right to know and the right to dissent. *That* is the freedom we desperately need. That is the kind of democracy we must demand from our leaders.

5.

When the "Good Guys" Censor

Article 19 of the International Covenant on Civil and Political Rights stipulates that "Everyone shall have the right to freedom of expression; this right shall include freedom to seek, receive and impart information and ideas of all kinds, regardless of frontiers, either orally, in writing or in print, in the form of art, or through any other media of his choice. "

A cautionary tale: On March 21, 2022, I was called and interviewed by *Sputnik* concerning the war in Ukraine. On March 22 the article was published, and I was provided with the digital link. When I tried to access the link, the server informed me: "This site can't be reached. **sputniknews.com.**" I was surprised, since I reside in Switzerland, which is a party to the ICCPR and obliged to guarantee the two rights enunciated in article 19:

1) the right to seek information and ideas, and

2) the right to impart and disseminate them.

When I sent the link to friends in the United States, they too could not access the link, although the United States is also a party to ICCPR. "Currently unable to access the article on Google's server in the U.S.," their error messages read.

Censorship is not just abstract—it takes on greater reality when it hits oneself.

What is going on? How extensive is it? Will we ever know how many voices are being silenced? How many crucial facts and explanations escape us?

Democracy can only function properly when citizens have access to all the information, perspectives and points of view, so that they can arrive at their own opinions. Freedom of expression is not confined to the right to echo whatever information and narratives we hear from our governments or from the "quality press," but encompasses the right to dissent from those views.

In order to build one's own judgment about facts and events, we need pluralistic access to news services.

It appears that censorship is being practiced both by governments that ostensibly declare themselves to be "democratic" and also by the private sector, including twitter, Facebook and YouTube. This kind of censorship is unworthy of democratic societies and should be condemned by the Office of the UN High Commissioner for Human Rights, by the UN Human Rights Council, by Amnesty International, Human Rights Watch and Reporters without Borders.

Censorship is exactly the wrong approach. Precisely now, in the midst of a military confrontation that threatens to escalate to endanger the entire planet and the survival of humanity, it is necessary to have a maximum of information and views, while stopping same is still possible. In particular it is necessary to have access to sedate analysis based on the UN Charter and international law. We must endeavor to understand the options, the nuances and the dissenting views in order to grasp the complexities of the problems, which are certainly not black and white. We must beware of joining "patriotic" bandwagons and make a conscious choice not to go down the path of Orwell's Ministry of Truth.

How can the EU criticise censorship in Russia and China, when European countries also practice censorship?

Here is the text of the censored *Sputnik* interview:

On 19 March 2003, Washington's Operation Shock and Awe started under a completely false pretext. You say that there has been no violation of the Nuremberg Principles as grave as the invasion, occupation and devastation of Iraq in 2003. What do you mean?

It was a veritable revolt against the Nuremberg Principles, international law and the international order, the cumulation of the crimes of aggression, war crimes and crimes against humanity—and all this in total impunity. The vastness of the operation, the viciousness of the bombardment, the destruction of world heritage sites and museums, the use of white phosphorus. depleted uranium weapons[23] and cluster bombs, widespread torture at Abu Ghraib, Mosul and other prisons including Guantánamo, the "extraordinary rendition" program—all this constituted "shock and awe" upon Iraqi victims, a demonstration of imperial power intended to convince the world of America's hegemony. It was not only the incompetent President George W. Bush and his hawkish neo-con advisors who were behind this atrocity. Bush ultimately pulled in the "coalition of the willing"—43 countries ostensibly committed to international law and human rights. Bush made them into accomplices in the assault against a hapless country and its population. The purpose was "regime change," to topple the Iraqi government of Saddam Hussein, to steal Iraqi oil and strengthen NATO's geopolitical presence in the Middle East. It was indeed "shock and awe," bringing about the collective devastation of a country that was not threatening anyone.

Let us not forget that the UN Security Council was already seized of the Iraqi situation since 1991, that there was no reason, no urgency to do anything against the government of Iraq that was already cooperating with the UN. Two United Nations inspectors were performing their job on the ground—systematically searching for weapons of mass destruction—and not finding any. Hans Blix and Mohamed El Baradei were both threatened by the United States to induce them to make a false finding that Saddam Hussein was in

---

23 John Catalinotto and Sara Flounders (Eds.), *Depleted Uranium: How the Pentagon Radiates Soldiers & Civilians with DU Weapons* (2nd ed.) (New York: International Action Center, 2005).

"material breach" of the relevant Security Council resolutions. This would have provided an "excuse," a mantle of legality for the U.S. to invade Iraq with the blessing of the Security Council. But Blix and ElBaradei did not deliver the magic words "material breach," and the UN had to withdraw its inspectors, because it became apparent that the U.S. would attack with or without approval by the Security Council. The whole operation was criminal and deliberate. It is a disgrace that 90% of the Western media supported "shock and awe" and disseminated the fake news and intelligence coming from Washington and London. Clearly George W. Bush and Tony Blair should have been sent before an international criminal tribunal. But no. There was total impunity for them and for the other "leaders" of democratic countries who participated in the bombing and looting. Only a Peoples' Tribunal at Kuala Lumpur could be convened, and those judges did convict both Bush and Blair.

According to the Quincy Institute for Responsible Statecraft, the Western media played a great role in whitewashing the illegal U.S. campaign. What's your take on the role of the Western media in world affairs, given that it still remains mute about the eight-year long genocide of Russian-speakers in Donbass, and peddling an untruthful and distorted narrative of Russian special operation today?

The Western media is complicit in NATO's crimes not only in Iraq, but also in Afghanistan, Libya and Syria. Our corporate media (I am an American citizen) engages in flagrant war propaganda and incitement to hatred—in 2003 against Iraq and the Iraqi people who supported Saddam Hussein, and today against, Russia and Russians, who are depicted as aggressors and gross violators of human rights. This Russophobic propaganda did not start in 2022—it has a long history going back to the 1950's and Joe McCarthy, going back to the demonization of Brezhnev and Andropov, and more recently of Vladimir Putin. The media systematically violates article 20(1) of the International Covenant on Civil and Political Rights, which prohibits war propaganda, and article 20(2) which prohibits incitement to racial hatred and violence. Of course, our corporate media are in the service of the hegemon and their job is to act as echo chambers for whatever the White House, the Pentagon, the CIA, M15 want to sell to the public. They participated in the demonization of Saddam Hussein and in the hysteria that accompanied the run-up to the invasion, which UN Secretary General Kofi Annan labelled an "illegal war" on repeated occasions. Our media does not only disseminate "fake news" and bogus arguments, it also suppresses inconvenient facts, including the massive violations of the 2014 and 2015 Minsk Agreements by Ukraine, the savage shelling of Lugansk and Donetsk, the destruction of hospitals and schools. Anyone who wants to be informed about what is happening in Ukraine must also consult *RT, Sputnik, CGTN, Asia Times, Global Times, Telesur, Prensa Latina* and "alternative media" like *The Grayzone, The Intercept, Consortium News,* and *Counterpunch.*

NATO countries unleashed wars and committed atrocities in Yugoslavia, Afghanistan, Iraq, Libya, Somalia and Syria. However, no one has been held responsible for this so far. Furthermore, in the eyes of the U.S. the ICC has no jurisdiction, no legitimacy, and no authority. What's your take on this situation?

I partly agree with the U.S. that the ICC has little or no authority and credibility. I disagree with the U.S. in that

I would wish to see a vigorous, objective and proactive ICC that would exercise jurisdiction not only over African leaders and military, but that would demonstrate the courage and independence to indict individuals from Western countries. In my opinion, George W. Bush, Tony Blair, Dick Cheney, Paul Wolfowitz, John Bolton, Barack Obama, Donald Trump, and Joe Biden all deserve being indicted—for war crimes and crimes against humanity, for the "collateral damage" caused by the indiscriminate use of drones, for the use of prohibited weapons and depleted uranium weapons with long-lasting radioactive impacts.[24] Indeed, the ICC will only have credibility when it decides to prosecute the big fish. Hitherto it seems that the ICC has largely served the interests of the Western countries and continues to operate as a smoke screen for the crimes of the West, focusing only on crimes committed by the "little fish."

Could one qualify NATO as a "criminal organization" for purposes of Article 9 of the Statute of Rome of 8 August 1945—the statute of the Nuremberg Tribunal? Is there ample evidence and necessary preconditions for it? How could this be done?

I would like to see Amnesty International and Human Rights Watch come out and call a spade a spade. I would like to see the UN Secretary General, the UN High Commissioner for Human Rights engage in more than just "peace" rhetoric, but to formulate an implementable plan that guarantees a security architecture for all countries in Europe and the world. I would like to see the Secretary General vindicate the purposes and principles of the UN Charter, including the sovereign

---

24 Catalinotto and Flounders (Eds.), *Depleted Uranium.*

equality of states and the right of self-determination of all peoples, including the peoples of Crimea and Donbas.

It is time to demand an end to impunity for the crime of aggression, war crimes and crimes against humanity. It is time to demand that the International Court of Justice declare in an Advisory Opinion that the eastern expansion of NATO entailed a "threat to international peace and security" for purposes of article 39 of the UN Charter and constituted a violation of article 2(4) of the Charter, which prohibits not only the use of force but also the threat of the use of force. How else can we describe the continuous expansion of NATO in violation of the assurances given to Gorbachev in 1989, 90 and 91? How else can we describe the massive rearmament of Ukraine with only one purpose—to intimidate Russia? NATO is certainly not a "defensive alliance"—at least not since the Warsaw Pact was dissolved in 1991. NATO has been trying to usurp the role of the UN Security Council, which has exclusive responsibility for keeping peace and security in the world. Of course, since the Security Council will never agree to impose a "Pax Americana" on the rest of the world, NATO unilaterally assumes the role of imperial policeman over the globe and establishes hundreds of military bases intended to encircle not only Russia, but China as well.

It should be the role of the International Criminal Court to investigate the war crimes and crimes against humanity committed by NATO countries in Yugoslavia, Afghanistan, Iraq, Libya and Syria. These crimes are documented not only in the publications of Wikileaks, but also in United Nations reports and countless eye-witness and victim testimonies. An Advisory Opinion of the International Court of Justice could look into the question whether the number and magnitude of these crimes qualify NATO as a "criminal organization" for purposes of article 9 of the London Agreement of 8 August 1945. Of course, there are serious problems with the concept of a "criminal organization," because we all believe in individual justice and reject the concept of collective guilt or guilt by association. It would be necessary to ensure the presumption of innocence of all members of a "criminal organization" and guarantee due process as provided for in article 14 of the International Covenant on Civil and Political Rights.

Questions concerning the crimes committed by NATO and NATO countries must be raised. Bearing in mind that NATO has such a long track record of war crimes and crimes against humanity, it is important that the historical record be established, and that civil society the world over reject the propaganda narratives and demand more transparency and accountability from the leaders of the U.S. and all NATO countries. Here is a task for the International Criminal Court—to examine whether the violations of articles 5, 6, 7 and 8 of the Statute of Rome by NATO countries justify calling NATO a "criminal organization." Bottom line: International law and international criminal law are by definition universal and must be enforced not only against little countries, but also against all members of the international community, objectively and without double standards.

6.

What and Whom to Believe

What do we believe? Whom *can* we believe and why? Is trust gratuitous, confined to "recognized authorities" or is it earned? Experience and "common sense" (that ever-so-rare attribute) may help us address these questions. But wait . . . how reliable are our evaluation tools? Even our rules of logic and rationality will fail us when the information supplied is false, incomplete or skewed.

Over millennia philosophers have pursued their quest for meaning, truth and justice, aware of the limitations imposed by the availability of empirical data and the psychological, societal and indeed governmental constraints of one's culture, heritage and political order. Whether we like it or not, we are children of our generation, and our language, social environment and education condition us to believe certain things and not others. It takes a certain temerity to jump over one's shadow and to attempt thinking outside the box, to test our own premises and consider extraneous perspectives. Are we sure that we ourselves are true and honest? Do we ever test our premises? Do we practice what we preach? Do we have good reason to trust the morals and intellectual honesty of our leaders?

Admittedly, human existence does not depend on philosophical reflection—live first, then philosophize—*primum vivere, deinde philosophari* (Cicero in a letter to his son Marcus). Undoubtedly, however, our perception of the spirituality of the universe and our conscious participation in the emotional landscape of our civilization can be immensely enriched by developing an awareness of our own selves—*nosce te ipsum* (the *Delphian γνῶθι σεαυτόν*), of our instincts and inclinations, preferences, prejudices. Such awareness enables us to put the cosmos in context and facilitates our understanding of chronologies, relationships, cause and effect. Life is so much more exciting when we connect with our own consciences, when we are free to evaluate persons and events and make up our own minds about people and events, rather than just joining bandwagons, echoing others, and lapsing into "groupthink."

Growing up means advancing from naïveté to critical judgment, keeping an open mind, questioning more, discarding old canards, acknowledging that we have been mistaken here and there, recognizing incongruities and rejecting cognitive dissonance.

Greek and Roman philosophers Socrates, Plato, Aristotle, Zeno, Cicero, Horace, Seneca, Juvenal—among others— endeavored to fathom the human psyche, our fears and beliefs. They also appreciated the wisdom of keeping a certain distance from what is happening around us, recognizing the importance of cool judgment, remaining impervious to surprise or disappointment. Indeed, a certain detachment and equanimity are sure values—they called it *"nil admirari."*

Don't get me wrong. None of these philosophers were nihilists—on the contrary, they recognized that it is crucial for the human being to have a set of beliefs and reference points. Especially, young people need to believe—albeit temporarily— in fantasies. Young people cannot and should not be "detached" but should instead go from surprise to surprise. Indeed, there is an added value to surprise—and young people should not be deprived of it. After all, they do need role models and should not be prematurely skeptical, blasé or cynical. Youth should feel the rush of adrenalin that goes with enthusiasm, the excitement of discovery, the euphoria of falling in love, the infatuation with infatuation, the illusion of heroism that buoys the heart and enriches imagination. Youth has a right to be in awe of Olympic achievements and individual achievers, should endeavor to imitate them, not be afraid of asking questions, testing established customs, making personal experiences—both good and bad— and most importantly, they should believe in something!

So make no mistake: while lessons learned confirm the Roman maxim *nil admirari*, this philosophical attitude is really something for post-adolescents. Only those who have experienced highs and lows can afford the temerity of questioning everything and believing only in what is properly substantiated.

As we grow older, we gradually evolve from innocence and credulity to a measure of realism and resignation. When we are twenty, we are full of optimism and purposefully look for heroes, halls of fame, iconographies of courage, virtuous causes.... By the time we are thirty, we begin to shed some illusions and honor fewer heroes. By the time we reach forty, we realize that most of our heroes were hardly knights in shining armour and that even they had their negative facets. By the time we are fifty, we start asking ourselves why we ever thought that a given author or politician or historical figure deserved our admiration, why were we so receptive to caricatures in the media and history books? Why did we trust the *Zeitgeist* and embrace the commercial and geopolitical propaganda served to us every day by the corporate media. By the time we make sixty, we realize that we have been programmed to believe in some politicians (and look down on others), manipulated to accept historical icons and certain convenient socio-economic myths (like the invisible hand of the market). By the time we are seventy, we have come to terms with the fact that we have been lied to for most of our lives—resigned to the fact that previous generations have gone through a similar process of indoctrination and disenchantment—as probably will be the fate of succeeding generations.

And if we ever survive to eighty or ninety—we may look back at the world and smile at it all in taciturn equanimity, aware that each generation must make its own experiences and arrive at its own value judgments, conscious that there is good in the bad and bad in the good, that we all have the "right to be wrong," that it is wise to forgive others—and ourselves, that vicarious living and "virtual reality" are only forms of escapism. Instead, for as long as we are alive, we owe it to ourselves, our families and friends to remain optimistic and engaged.

If we have no more heroes, if we no longer believe in Camelot, let us at least continue to admire the exuberant beauty of the universe, the splendour of our fauna and flora, the elegance of the Vanessa Atalanta butterfly, the ephemeral poetry of sunrise and sunset, the metaphysical truth of Bach and Beethoven! There is plenty to believe in!

7.

What Is Patriotism?

During my six years as UN independent expert for international order, I experienced more than the average level of animosity, mobbing, assaults on my personal integrity and ethics, distortion of my message, deliberate misquotation, below-the-belt insults, actionable defamation, and even a couple of death threats.

It is ironic to be accused of being on the payroll of China, Cuba, Russia or Venezuela. No government or foreign intelligence service ever approached me, much less offered money, although my own country's CIA did try to recruit me as a mole on two occasions. While I believe in the U.S. Marine Corps's motto "Semper fidelis" (always faithful), I am simply not gifted to work as a spy. The reality is that my independence and commitment to objective and ethical investigations, wherever they may lead me, never brought me a cent from any government, foundation, lobby, non-governmental organization. It did not bring me honorary doctorates, prizes and awards. Whereas all of my published op-eds have been offered free of charge, I have had to forgo potentially lucrative interviews—because CNN and BBC do not seek my opinion.

As a retired UN rapporteur, I have endeavored to remain informed and active. From time to time I give interviews and publish op-eds, e.g. concerning NATO, Uyghurs, President Biden's "Summit for Democracy," the *contra legem* rulings of UK tribunals in the case of Julian Assange, etc.. This exercise of my right of freedom of opinion and expression has brought me more insults than anticipated and in one particular assault on my convictions—I have been called "unpatriotic" and even a "traitor."

Reflecting on this surge in social media hostility, I jotted down some thoughts on the meaning of patriotism, loyalty to one's country, community, values and human dignity.

Of course, patriotism means different things to different people. For me it entails citizen solidarity in promoting justice at home and resisting official lies, apologetics, euphemisms, rejecting the tyranny of governments and the phoniness of political correctness.

Love of country requires a commitment to truth and readiness to counter "fake news" and skewed political narratives. Internationally, patriotism means averting harm from one's country by pro-actively seeking dialogue and compromise, so as to contribute to peace and justice—*pax et iustitia.*

Some adolescents and young soldiers think that patriotism can be boiled down to the formula "my country right or wrong," and thus unwittingly risk becoming cannon fodder, the victims of warmongers and war-profiteers, who do not risk their own skins and let others die for their profits.

Patriotism must not be confused with chauvinism or jingoism. It is a positive value, aimed at advancing justice for one's community—it is not xenophobic. Patriotism does not entail blind loyalty to the "establishment." It requires civic responsibility, asking question, making sure that our democratically elected officials do not morph into tyrants.

Patriotism cannot and must not require a knee-jerk reaction. This fundamentally flawed formula can only be described as an irresponsible cop-out, which only invites governments to abuse our trust, waste our tax dollars in foreign interventions, breach our privacy through illegal surveillance, and commit any number of geopolitical crimes.

A true patriot says, "Not in my name." A true patriot weighs the pros and cons of government policies and demands access to information, freedom of opinion and expression, the emblematic first Amendment to the U.S. Constitution, which our country claims to be the leading champion of, and demands transparency and accountability from government.

If pursued by all, freedom of information and expression would ensure that our countries are indeed on the path to peace and justice. Horace's noble-sounding maxim *dulce et decorum est pro patria mori* (it is sweet and appropriate to die for one's country) must be recast in constructive terms: It is sweet to *live for* one's country, it is honorable to contribute to a just and harmonious society! Indeed, that is what Cicero meant with *caritas patriae.*

Who qualifies as a patriot? For me: every citizen who takes democracy seriously and demands truth and ethical behavior from the authorities. Among patriots in the 21st century, I count the whistle-blowers who uncover corruption, political scams and criminal activities by both the government and the private sector. They have been the gatekeepers of the social order. Surely Edward Snowden is a patriot, as he risked life and career because of his conscience. We can learn more in his riveting book, *Permanent Record.* We all owe him a huge debt of gratitude. He, together with Julian Assange, deserve the Nobel Prize for Peace.

By contrast, who is *not* a patriot? Every opportunist who advances his/her career at the expense of the common good, anyone who manipulates public opinion through sensationalism, evidence-free allegations, sabre-rattling and ends up dragging the country and its young soldiers into criminal wars and misery for all sides. The security of everybody has been seriously compromised by these criminal war hawks, who sometimes are revered and hailed by the media as "patriots."

Recently I have been criticized for publishing articles and interviews with *Truthout, CounterPunch, RT, CGTN, Asia Times, Global Times, Telesur, PressTV.* I have been asked why is it that I do not publish also in *The New York Times* or *Washington Post?* My laconic response reflects the state of censorship in our "free press." Indeed, the mainstream media have never cared to interview me or invite me to write an article, not even during my six years as UN rapporteur.

The impact of this deliberate suppression of opinion affects not only me, it also impinges on the rights of the broader public to know what an international civil servant and UN rapporteur has to say about a particular issue. Whether he is right or wrong is another matter. But all views should be given a chance in the marketplace of ideas. The reality is that only those rapporteurs who sing the desired song are interviewed or invited to write op-eds. Dozens of my proposed op-eds were rejected by several mainstream outlets.

Add this to the "cancel culture"—the growing list of private-sector censorship and suppression of independent views. Who knows how often other UN Rapporteurs have been mobbed and insulted as I have been. Of course, many rapporteurs avoid social ostracism by toeing the line and thus staying out of controversy. This may also explain why so many in society have lost faith in the United Nations as a vector of truth, change and effective promotion of human rights.

In the context of the Ukraine war I published several articles in Swiss journals including *Zeit-Fragen, Horizons et Debats, Current Concerns, Schweizer Standpunkt, Point de Vue Suisse,* and *Zeitgeschehen im Fokus.* I received much positive feedback, precisely because the readership perceived me as a responsible Swiss citizen who wants to alert the Swiss public to certain facts and nuances that the mainstream media systematically suppress. They thanked me for sharing my knowledge and expertise with the broader Swiss public. In this sense, I consider myself as both a U.S. and a Swiss patriot.

Patriotism is not just applauding the leadership of our government and our institutions; it also requires alertness and constructive dissent. Conscientious objection, a right protected under article 18 of the International Covenant on Civil and Political Rights, can be an important manifestation of patriotism, e.g. when politicians stampede into war and chaos.

Patriotism is more than waving flags and joining bandwagons, denouncing enemies and howling with the wolves. It is not populism, blind obedience to the government and its military machine, not cheering purported "heroes" and swimming with the mainstream. Patriotism means genuine love of a country's population, concern for everyone's welfare, especially the most vulnerable. It entails respect for a country's constitution, rule of law, values and traditions, a commitment to truthfulness and intellectual honesty. Sometimes It may require significant economic and personal sacrifice. It demands responsibility from each and every one of us, awareness of the issues and a conscious effort to contribute to the commonweal with courage and perseverance. It should be the credo of every citizen.

THE
WEAPONIZATION
OF HUMAN RIGHTS

8.

A Litmus Test for Democracy

President Joe Biden's "Summit for Democracy" of December 9–10, 2021 should first agree on a definition of what democracy means. Whereas etymologically we know that the definition of democracy means rule by the people, instinctively we feel that people power must be more than a slogan, that it must be concretized by genuine public participation in the conduct of public affairs.

There are, of course, many manifestations or "models" of democracy, exercised nationally as well as locally in provinces and communities. The spectrum of democratic governance goes from direct democracy by way of citizen power of initiative and the possibility to challenge legislation by way of referenda, to participatory democracy through public meetings and voting on specific issues by ballot (or even show of hands!), to representative democracy through the election of parliamentarians with specific mandates, to presidential democracy by electing a president with wide-ranging powers.

As a Swiss citizen, I recognize the benefits of the semi-direct democracy practiced in Switzerland. Indeed, I vote in every single election and referendum, and actively participate in the public debate that precedes them, and in this way, I feel that my opinion counts. As also an American citizen I vote in every congressional and presidential election every two years. However, on the important issues I feel that there is no genuine choice given to the electorate, because the two parties converge precisely on those issues where there must be change. Because there is hardly a possibility to influence domestic or international policy, I and many other Americans feel disenfranchised. We suffer from endemic democratic deficits.

What criteria can be used to assess the level of democratic governance in any given country? What measuring stick can we use? To what extent can citizens genuinely influence governmental policies? Surely the correlation between the will of the people and the governmental policies that affect their lives is crucial.

What are some preliminary conditions that should be met? As a Litmus test we should ask:

1. Does the political establishment consisting of local and central governments pro-actively inform citizens about proposed legislation and options?

2. Are citizens asked what their priorities are, what they want to change?

3. Are citizens regularly consulted on their needs and preferences?

4. Do citizens have access to all necessary information, access to official documents, access to truth, so that they can judiciously exercise democratic rights?

5. Does the government practice censorship or suppress key information, does the government indoctrinate in order to "manufacture consent"?

6. Is there a pluralistic media that separates reporting of facts from editorial opinion?

7. Does the private-sector media engage in censorship or suppression of key information preventing the citizens to have a realistic opportunity to understand and choose between policy options?

8. Do the citizens have realistic opportunity to designate the candidates for election and can they vote freely without fearing reprisals?

Once these preliminary questions have been sorted out, we can formulate specific issues of importance to the daily lives of citizens and explore to what extent citizens have some control over decisions taken by the authorities. What is the level of government secrecy? How often are political scandals covered-up? Do transparency and accountability actually exist? We can then rate democratic governance by addressing a number of concrete questions that would reveal whether governments are in tune with their populations or whether there is some kind of "disconnect."

Let us review the world we live in and how certain political decisions were made, the consequences of which we bear and which we feel impotent to reverse. For instance, were these major issues ever raised in any significant manner by its political figures and institutions as worthy of consultation with and approval by the citizenry of the country? Issues such as:

1. the proportion of the discretionary budget that should be spent on the military

2. the establishment of the National Security Agency and its worldwide surveillance of persons and companies;

3. the continued persecution of whistle-blowers;

4. the "bailouts" given to the banks after the financial melt-down of 2007/8;

5. the establishment of tax havens and the protection given to them by law;

6. the CIA practices of targeted assassination;

7. the torture practices in Abu Ghraib, Mosul and Guantánamo;

8. the "extraordinary rendition" program;

9. the imposition of killer sanctions on Cuba, Nicaragua, Syria, Venezuela;

10. the decision to go to war: The Vietnam war, NATO's assault on Yugoslavia in 1999? NATO's assault on Libya 2011, NATO's assault on Syria;

11. the expansion of NATO to Russia's borders in violation of the agreements made in 1989 and 1990 with Soviet President Gorbachev;

12. fracking, large-scale mining, oil prospecting and logging in indigenous lands, e.g. in Alaska;

13. the subsidies given to oil and gas industries;

14. the subsidies given to nuclear industries;

15. the practice of vaccine hoarding.

To the extent that the populations of many countries would have to answer all of the above questions in the negative, because they were never properly informed and consulted, because they were never asked "do you want peace or war?" it would appear that there is a serious disconnect between people and governments.

Bearing in mind that many Western countries are advocates of "competition," it would be interesting to see how these countries actually compete in terms of democratic governance. One could anticipate that some participants in the "Summit for democracy" would probably end up with rather low scores. We would have to conclude that many "democratic" governments actually practice fake democracy based on fake news and fake law.

At its core Biden's "Democracy Summit" has a public relations and propagandistic purpose: To try to convince the world that the U.S. is the paragon of democracy and that our model is the best. This conflicts with General Assembly Resolution 60/1, the Outcome Document of the 2005 World Conference. Paragraph 135 of the Resolution clearly states:

We reaffirm that democracy is a universal value based on the freely expressed will of people to determine their own political, economic, social and cultural systems and their full participation in all aspects of their lives.

We also reaffirm that while democracies share common features, there is no single model of democracy, that it does not belong to any country or region, and reaffirm the necessity of due respect for sovereignty and the right of self-determination. We stress that democracy, development and respect for all human rights and fundamental freedoms are interdependent and mutually reinforcing.

Bottom line: a democratic government must inform, consult, and give real options to the citizens. The way in which the Western model of "democracy" is practiced does not take the human being and his/her dignity seriously. Thus, in many countries, democracy is more of a façade than reality. Alas, most countries attending the "Summit for democracy" will fail the litmus test.

9.

Reflections on Genocide

with Prof. Richard Falk

The misuse of the word genocide is disdainful toward relatives of the victims of the Armenian massacres, the Holocaust, the Rwandan genocide, the Nanking genocide—and as well a disservice to both history, law, and the prudent conduct of international relations. We already knew that we were adrift in an ocean of fake news. It is far more dangerous to discover that we are also at risk of being immersed in the turbulent waters of "fake law." We must push back with a sense of urgency. Such a development is not tolerable.

We thought that Biden's election would spare us from menacing corruptions of language of the sort disseminated by Donald Trump, John Bolton, and Mike Pompeo. We thought that we would no longer be subjected to evidence-free allegations, post-truth, and cynical concoctions of fact. It now seems we were wrong.

We recall Pompeo's bragging about the usefulness of lying, we listened to his incendiary allegations against Cuba and Nicaragua, his outlandish claims that Hezbollah was in Venezuela, his antics on behalf of Trump—all in the name of MAGA.

Donald Trump and Mike Pompeo did not succeed in making America great again. They did succeed in lowering the already low opinion that the world had of America as a country that played by the rules set forth in international law. A decisive development in this downward spiral was George W. Bush's megacrime—the unprovoked invasion and devastation of Iraq, which UN Secretary-General Kofi Annan called an "illegal war" on more than one occasion. We observed Barack Obama's involvement in the destruction of Libya, given a bitter resonance by Hillary Clinton's unspeakable words on Qaddafi's demise uttered with imperial glee: "We came, we saw, he died."[25] We cannot forget Trump's criminal economic sanctions and financial blockades punishing whole societies in the midst of a crippling pandemic. These were crimes against humanity committed in our name. Such sanctions reminded us of merciless medieval sieges of towns, aimed at starving whole populations into submission. We think back to the one million civilian deaths resulting from Germany blockading Leningrad 1941–44.

No, to make America great again, it seems perverse to suppose that this can come about by continuing to behave as an international bully, threatening and beating up on entire peoples. No, in order to make America respected and admired in the world we can and should start by reviving the legacy of Eleanor Roosevelt, by rediscovering the spirit and spirituality of the Universal Declaration of Human Rights, and more broadly re-enacting the peace-oriented humanism of John F. Kennedy.

We can and should be demanding more from Joe Biden and Antony Blinken. Evidence-free allegations of "genocide" in Xinjiang, China, are unworthy of any country, and most of all, of the country that wants to act as the prime international champion of human rights. Raphael Lemkin would turn in his grave if he learned that the crime of "genocide" has been so crassly instrumentalized to beat the drums of Sinophobia. The sudden flurry of United States interest in the fate of the Uyghur people seems less motivated by compassion or the protection of human rights than lifted from the most cynical pages of the Machiavellian playbook of geopolitics.

Genocide is a well-defined term in international law—in the 1948 Genocide Convention and Article 6 of the Rome Statute. The most respected international tribunals have separately agreed that proof of the crime of genocide depends on an

---

25 Hillary Clinton, "We Came, We Saw, He Died" (Gaddafi), YouTube video, 0:37, posted December 17, 2011 by NTCNATO, https://www.youtube.com/watch?v=FmIRYvJQeHM.

extremely convincing presentation of factual evidence, including documentation of an *intent* to destroy in whole or in part a national, ethnic, racial or religious group. The International Criminal Tribunal for the former Yugoslavia, the International Criminal Tribunal for Rwanda, the International Court of Justice—all have endeavored to provide authoritative tests of "intent," treating intent as the essential element in the crime of genocide.

This jurisprudence is what should be guiding our politicians in reaching prudent conclusions as to whether there exist credible grounds to put forward accusations of genocide, given its inflammatory effects. We should be asking whether the factual situation is clouded, calling for an independent international investigation followed by further action if deemed appropriate. In nuclear-armed world, we should be extremely careful before making such an accusation.

Mike Pompeo's allegation that China was committing genocide in Xinjiang was unsupported by even a hint of evidence. It was a particularly irresponsible example of ideological posturing at its worst, and besides, an embrace of reckless geopolitics. That is why it is so shocking to us that the 2021 U.S. State Department Human Rights Report repeats the "genocide" charge in its Executive Summary yet doesn't even bother to mention such a provocative charge in the body of the report. This is an irresponsible, unreasonable, unprofessional, counter-productive, and above all, dangerously incendiary allegation, which could easily spiral out of control if China should choose to respond in kind. China would be on firmer ground than Pompeo or the State Department if it were to accuse the United States of "continuing genocide" against the First Nations of the Americas, the Cherokee, Sioux, Navajo, and many other tribal nations. We can only imagine the outrage if China had been the first to put forward loose talk about genocide.

By making unsubstantiated claims the U.S. Government is seriously undermining its own authority and the credibility it needs to revive its role as global leader. To play this constructive international role is not on display by "weaponizing" human rights against China—or Russia. Instead, a foreign policy dedicated to the genuine promotion of human rights would call for international cooperation in conducting reliable investigations of gross violations of human rights and international crimes, wherever they occur—whether it be in India, Egypt, China, Russia, Turkey, Saudi Arabia, Myanmar, Yemen, Brazil, Colombia. We would even hope that Biden's Washington would be sufficiently committed as to be receptive to investigations undertaken in response to allegations of violations against the United States of America and its closest allies in Europe and elsewhere.

The Orwellian corruption of language by U.S. Government officials, their double standards, the dissemination of fake news by the mainstream media, including the "quality press" and CNN, self-anointed as "the most trusted name in news," are eroding our self-respect. Indeed, the manipulation of public opinion undermines our democracy as we succumb to belief in the exaggerated wrongs of others that give an added bite to our hostile propaganda and is leading the world to the very edge of a forbidding geopolitical precipice, and in the process, heightening the prospects of a new cold war—or worse.

The Biden Administration at the very least should show respect for the American people and for international law by stopping its cheapening of the meaning of the word "genocide" and ceasing to treat human rights as geopolitical tools of conflict. Such irresponsible behavior may soothe the nerves of Trumpists, and fashion a façade of unity based on portraying China as the new "evil empire," but it's a foreign policy ploy that should be rejected as a recipe for global disaster.

10.

The Pseudo–Uyghur Tribunal

On December 9, 2021, the anniversary of the adoption by the General Assembly of the Genocide Convention in 1948, the so-called Uyghur Tribunal in London declared that China had committed genocide against Uygur and other ethnic minorities.

What kind of a tribunal was this, and what credibility does it have? In past decades we have seen that some People's tribunals like the Bertrand Russell Tribunal on Vietnam (1966), the Kuala Lumpur Tribunal on war crimes in Iraq (2011) or the Lelio Basso Tribunal on the genocide against the Tamils (2013) can be useful institutions, especially when the corporate media fails to inform the public about war crimes and crimes against humanity, downplays the number or victims or whitewashes the perpetrators.

Peoples' tribunals are legitimate because they reflect a malaise resulting from the manipulation of public opinion by the mainstream media, and constitute a spontaneous protest against the crime of silence by governments and media. Such tribunals constitute a form of transitional justice that challenges legalism and the judicial monopoly of the state. They are necessary where the global order has failed to punish war crimes and crimes against humanity, e.g., in Vietnam, Afghanistan and Iraq.

By contrast, there are also political tribunals that are constituted to advance and corroborate the geopolitical agendas of certain countries. No one will claim that the allegations against China concerning Uyghurs have been ignored or covered up by the press. On the contrary, for years, U.S. and UK politicians have been making evidence-free accusations,[26] which the main-

---

26 Jeffrey D. Sachs, "The Xinjiang Genocide Allegations Are Unjustified," April 20, 2021, *Project Syndicate,* https://www.project-syndicate.org/commentary/ biden-should-withdraw-unjustified-xinjiang-genocide-allegation-by-jeffrey-d-sachs-

stream media, including the BBC, have dutifully reported and magnified. A "Tribunal" like the Uyghur Tribunal has a very specific purpose—not to enlighten the public but to feed into a well-orchestrated campaign.

This UK-based "tribunal," launched on September 3, 2020 with assistance from a non-governmental organization, the Coalition for Genocide Response, is a partisan exercise that aims to manipulate public opinion against an economic rival—China.

Who finances the propaganda exercise? It is public knowledge that the tribunal is financed by the "World Uyghur Congress," a "regime-change" pseudo-organization supported by the United States National Endowment for Democracy. This World Uyghur Congress is also associated with the Eastern Turkestan Islamist Movement—an organization on the UN terrorist list, which is guilty of terrorist activities in China's Xinjiang Uygur Autonomous Region.

Since the surge in agitation against China under Donald Trump, the Chinese government has provided answers and evidence to the almost surrealistic allegations of "genocide" in Xinjiang. China has opened its doors to the UN High Commissioner for Human Rights, Michelle Bachelet, who will visit the region in May 2022.[27] There can be no objection against

---

and-william-schabas-2021-04.

27 Stephanie Nebehay, "U.N. rights boss to visit China in May, including Xinjiang, but activists demand report," *Reuters,* March 8, 2022, https://www.reuters.com/world/china/un-rights-boss-bachelet-says-china-visit-agreed-may-including-xinjiang-2022-03-08/.

The High Commissioner's mission to China constitutes a positive example of confidence-building. HC Bachelet issued a very balanced statement on her mission, in which she lauds the cooperation of the Chinese authorities and the opportunity to visit sites in the Xinjiang Uygur Autonomous Region and speak with government critics and non-governmental organizations. Most importantly, Bachelet reports that a working group has been established to coordinate cooperation with OHCHR and offer advisory services and technical assistance.

In her statement at the end of the Mission, on May 28, 2022 [see "Statement by UN High Commissioner for Human Rights Michelle Bachelet after official visit to China," https://www.ohchr.org/en/statements/2022/05/statement-un-high-commissioner-human-rights-michelle-bachelet-after-official] Bachelet highlighted:

a truly impartial investigation of charges of "forced labor," but the investigators must be objective and in good faith.

Whoever has followed developments around the Uyghur tribunal and the disinformation in the corporate media realizes that the UK tribunal was set up to arrive at a certain conclusion, namely genocide and that the "trial" was conducted on a "presumption of guilt," as the spokesperson of the Chinese Mission to the UN in Geneva, Liu Yuyin, noted in a statement. Therefore, it would not deserve our attention, except that it is a propaganda tool which, insofar as the "narrative managers" in the corporate media in the U.S., UK and EU will be instrumentalizing it to

---

"In the Xinjiang Uyghur Autonomous Region, I have raised questions and concerns about the application of counter-terrorism and de-radicalisation measures and their broad application—particularly their impact on the rights of Uyghurs and other predominantly Muslim minorities. While I am unable to assess the full scale of the VETCs, I raised with the Government the lack of independent judicial oversight of the operation of the program, the reliance by law enforcement officials on 15 indicators to determine tendencies towards violent extremism, allegations of the use of force and ill treatment in institutions, and reports of unduly severe restrictions on legitimate religious practices. During my visit, the Government assured me that the VETC system has been dismantled. I encouraged the Government to undertake a review of all counter terrorism and deradicalization policies to ensure they fully comply with international human rights standards, and in particular that they are not applied in an arbitrary and discriminatory way. Before coming to China, I heard from some Uyghur families now living abroad who have lost contact with their loved ones. In my discussions with the authorities, I appealed to them to take measures to provide information to families as a matter of priority."

Following Bachelet's visit, a number of pseudo-NGOs protested, because Bachelet did not "condemn" China. For these operatives in the service of the U.S. and EU, the only function of a High Commissioner is to engage in "naming and shaming" and toeing the Washington line. See Helen Davidson, "Fury at UN human rights chief over 'whitewash' of Uyghur repression," The Guardian, June 9, 2022, https://www.theguardian.com/world/2022/jun/09/fury-at-un-human-rights-chief-over-whitewash-of-uyghur-repression, and "UN Human Rights Chief concludes failed visit to China, misses historic opportunity," International Service for Human Rights, May 29, 2022, https://ishr.ch/latest-updates/un-rights-chief-concludes-failed-visit-to-china-misses-historic-opportunity/. I issued a media statement defending the integrity of the High Commissioner and the importance of her mission and uploaded it on my blog: https://dezayasalfred.wordpress.com/2022/06/09/media-statement-pseudo-ngos-unhappy-with-high-commissioners-visit-to-china/.

pursue their Sino-phobic disinformation about Xinjiang and on-going hate speech campaign against China, runs counter to and impugns the otherwise laudable use of Peoples' Tribunals under circumstances that call for their use.

It is not entirely clear why a legal expert like Sir Geoffrey Nice, a former prosecutor at the International Criminal Tribunal for the Former Yugoslavia, would lend his good name to this. In any event, the judgment ultimately rendered is not exactly what we have read in the boulevard press, which is sensationalist and eager to spread scandal.

While the tribunal reviewed the five acts of genocide listed in article 2 of the 1948 Genocide Convention, it did reject four of them, observing that there is no evidence of genocidal intent. But then the tribunal went on to examine the fourth criterion of imposing measures to prevent reproduction and deems it sufficient to consider it genocide.[28]

There is really no case law on prevention of reproduction, and the Uyghur situation is hardly a candidate for such a momentous finding, because the purpose of the Chinese measures is not and never was to "destroy in whole or in part" the Uyghur group by suppression of births but reflects a general population-control strategy in a country that already has 1.4 billion human beings.

Such a measure may be criticized, but it seems to be within the domestic jurisdiction of a state that is concerned about the well-being of the entire population and not targeting a specific population. Prima vista this does not appear unusual because of the very high birth rate in the region. Notwithstanding the Chinese measures, the Uygur population continues to grow more rapidly than the population in the rest of China.

So, where is the genocide? There is no legal authority or precedent to claim that trying to reduce a very high birth rate

28 Scott Horton, "Gareth Porter on the Misleading Data Behind Uyghur Genocide Claims," *The Scott Horton Show,* February 19, 2021, podcast video 40:55, https://scotthorton.org/interviews/2-19-21-gareth-porter-on-the-misleading-data-behind-uyghur-genocide-claims/.

to something more modest is something contemplated under article 2(d) of the Genocide Convention. Does this make good sense? Any solid international lawyer would consider such an interpretation of the Convention as nonsensical.

A possible explanation for this finding by the tribunal is that while it could not see the validity of the genocide argument in general, it could not bring itself to reject it altogether either. By developing this bizarre spin, the tribunal managed to save face because, with the Sino-phobic environment surrounding the proceedings, a complete acquittal of China would have been unthinkable.

The "judgment" made by this tribunal is fundamentally flawed because it is partly based on fake information, extrapolations, hyperbole, and blithely ignores that core principle of all tribunals—*audiatur et altera pars*—which means not only listening to all sides of an issue, including documentation made public by the government of China, but pro-actively seeking all pertinent information and evaluating it in good faith. Even the internet provides abundant information that contradicts the tribunal's judgment.

We should all be concerned about the Orwellian corruption of language, the double standards, and the manipulation of public opinion, which undermine our democracies and erode our self-respect and capacity for understanding current issues. We must be very careful that such hostile propaganda does not lead the world down the geopolitical precipice.

11.

Citius, Altius, Fortius:
The Political Games around the
Beijing Olympics

"Faster, higher, stronger." This is the motto of the Olympic Games proposed by the French Baron de Coubertin, who in 1896 revived the ancient Greek games (8th century BC to 4th century AD) as a program of moral beauty. The modern Olympic games exult in the aesthetics of sports without borders, committed to the idea that the most important thing is not to win, but to participate, just as life is the journey, not the destination, and success is found not in the ephemeral triumph but in the honorable competition. Sports contribute to peace and understanding, precisely in the same sense as the UN Charter and the UNESCO Constitution.

The Olympic flag which rises at every Olympic event and flies over the headquarters of the International Olympic Committee at Lausanne, Switzerland, has five intertwining rings which represent the five continents of Planet Earth and their fraternal interdependence.

Perhaps better than any other human activity, sports illustrates the aspiration of all human beings to go beyond apparent limits, to go faster, climb higher, be stronger. In a way it is the unwritten credo of humanity: the desire for progress, for moving forward, doing things better, both individually and collectively. Watching the Olympics shows us what the human being is capable of—and gives us a sense of wonderment and humility.

These common aspirations of humanity are reflected in the UN Charter, which is committed to development through international cooperation, as laid down in articles 55–60 (Chapter IX). The Charter is inspired by an optimistic vision of a better world based on cooperation, multilateralism, a holistic approach to human rights, and, yes, a form of constructive competition, as we experience in sports.

Again and again, we witness how sports have a unique potential to advance friendship across borders and manifest common human traits such as love of beauty and coherence, the excitement of discovery and surprise, the explosion of laughter and joy, the pursuit of that elusive satisfaction that great achievement can provide.

Unfortunately, the Olympic ideal has been increasingly politicized. Again and again some countries pretend that they can instrumentalize sports for their own geopolitical ambitions. These countries betray the humanistic credo of the Olympic games when they weaponize sports to denounce and exclude others, instead of endeavoring to build bridges of friendship, understanding and inclusion.

The 2022 Beijing Winter Olympics have been denounced by some countries as the "genocide games," based on malicious and mendacious evidence-free allegations of human rights violations in the Chinese province of Xinjiang. A few countries have engaged in a "diplomatic boycott" of the Beijing Olympics, among them the United States, Canada, the United Kingdom, Australia and India (because a Chinese torchbearer had served during the 2020 border clashes in the Himalayas).

There is an old saying that people in glass houses should not throw stones. Similarly, we also remember the admonition by Christ to those who were about to lapidate a woman: "He that is without sin among you, let him first cast a stone at her."[29] As we know from the Universal Periodic Reports before the UN Human Rights Council, all of these five countries have major human rights problems. They are not without sin.

The United States has a history of aggression against many countries in all five continents.[30] And in its dealings with the

---

29 John 8:7.

30 See Stephen Kinzer's revealing book, *Overthrow: America's Century of*

Afro-American population, the Unites States has a long history of slavery, lynching, segregation, discrimination, police brutality (see the Black Lives Matter movement). What is less known is the history of the destruction of the ten million original inhabitants of the North American continent, the Crees, Cherokees, Sioux, Dakotas, Pequots and Navajos. In his 1964 book, *Why We Can't Wait,* Martin Luther King, Jr., wrote:

> Our nation was born in genocide when it embraced the doctrine that the original American, the Indian, was an inferior race. Even before there were large numbers of Negroes on our shores, the scar of racial hatred had already disfigured colonial society. From the sixteenth century forward, blood flowed in battles over racial supremacy. We are perhaps the only nation which tried as a matter of national policy to wipe out its indigenous population. Moreover, we elevated that tragic experience into a noble crusade. Indeed, even today we have not permitted ourselves to reject or to feel remorse for this shameful episode. Our literature, our films, our drama, our folklore all exalt it.[31]

These words are tough to hear, but unfortunately very true. That is perhaps why this aspect of Martin Luther King's legacy is systematically ignored by the media, why it is not taught in high schools and universities. I sincerely hope that one day history will give credit to Dr. King for taking up the cause of the indigenous as well. Unfortunately, nearly sixty years after Dr. King wrote those words, racism against indigenous Americans persists, and many do not forget the signs that hung in South Dakota stores, in Arizona near the Navajo "Reservation" and in

---

Regime Change from Hawaii to Iraq (New York: Henry Holt & Co., 2006).

31 Dr. Martin Luther King Jr., *Why We Can't Wait* (New York: New American Library, Signet Classics, 2000), 120.

so many other places in the American West: "No dogs or Indians allowed."

Canada, similarly, engaged in genocide against its indigenous populations. The few remaining indigenous were put into "residential schools" to be de-Indianized. As Duncan Campbell Scott, Superintendent of the Department of Indian Affairs, once wrote: "I want to get rid of the Indian problem [. . .] Our objective is to continue until there is not a single Indian in Canada that has not been absorbed into the body politic and there is no Indian question." One may add that Campbell added insult to injury by referring to an "Indian" problem, when he meant the right of identity of the Original Nations of Canada—inter alia, the Algonquin, the Cree, the Tlingit, the Mi'kmaq, the Mohawk, the Oneida, and the Squamish—none of them inhabitants of the *Indian* Sub-continent! Perhaps the best book in the field is by Tamara Starblanket, *Suffer the Little Children. Genocide, Indigenous Nations and the Canadian State.*[32]

Australia has a similar sad history of genocide against the native aborigines of the Australian Continent and Tasmania. At least since the Apology Resolution by Prime Minister Kevin Rudd in 2008, a gradual awareness of the problem has actually made its way into the mainstream media.

The United Kingdom has an equally dismal human rights record through the centuries. The history of the oppression of the Indian subcontinent by the British Empire, the exploitation of the huge territory that today encompasses India, Pakistan, Bangladesh and Sri Lanka would fill many volumes. Most pertinent in the discussion about the UK diplomatic boycott of the Beijing Olympics are the crimes of the British Empire against China. Indeed, in 1839–42 and again in 1853 the British Empire waged aggressive wars against the China in order to force the Chinese to buy British opium. These obscene "Opium Wars" had their origin in the fact that Britain was a Narco-empire and Queen Victoria was a Narco-queen, who forcefully sold opium

---

32 Clarity Press, Atlanta, Ga., 2018.

to China to resolve the UK imbalance of trade, since the Brits coveted Chinese silks, porcelains and other luxury goods. Out of the Chinese defeat and humiliation by Britain emerged the colony of Hong Kong, which China only recovered in 1997. That is yet another reason why—when the UK today criticizes China because of its policies in Hong Kong—reasonable people should remember that the UK had no right to have been in Hong Kong in the first place and that the UK should instead pay trillions of pounds to the Chinese in compensation for the outrages committed by the British Empire and by the United Kingdom in Hong Kong for a century and a half.

Finally, we come to India, which has oppressed, among others, the Kashmiri people since the Partition of the Indian Sub-Continent, oppressed them, exploited them and committed genocide against them. The reign of terror against Kashmir continues, notwithstanding strong criticism in the UN Human Rights Council and countless side events held at the United Nations demanding a referendum as envisaged in Security Council resolution 47 of 1948.

Why, then, this "diplomatic boycott" of the Beijing Olympics in particular? Would it not be more in keeping with the spirit of the Olympic movement and with the spirit of all world religions if we would call for a "truce," a *Treuga Dei*—at least for the duration of the games?

12.

Economic Sanctions Kill

The international community is committed to advancing the enjoyment of all human rights by all persons in all countries. This noble goal, morally enshrined in the Universal Declaration of Human Rights and legally enshrined in the ten core human rights treaties, can only be achieved through international solidarity and cooperation.

The international community is also bound to advance the foundational purposes of the UN, namely the promotion of local, regional, and international peace and development. In order to achieve these goals strategies should be developed, so that a democratic and equitable international order can emerge that brings prosperity and stability while respecting the sovereignty of states, their right to choose their socio-economic systems and modalities, and the right of self-determination of peoples.

The Office of the UN High Commissioner for Human Rights has shown that its Advisory Services and Technical Assistance are effective in strengthening democracy, the rule of law and state institutions. One example: The opening of an OHCHR bureau in Caracas, Venezuela, in 2019, which I strongly advocated when I was the first UN rapporteur to visit Venezuela in 21 years, represents a significant step in coordinating the assistance of UN agencies including UNDP, UNHCR, UNICEF, UNEP, WHO, ILO and FAO.

Bearing in mind that the United Nations Charter is akin to a world constitution, we should endeavor to ensure that international action is based on multilateralism and that domestic law and practice conforms with that constitution. History shows that international peace and the welfare of nations are threatened by unilateralism, including by the imposition of unilateral coercive measures against other countries, most frequently against geopolitical or geoeconomics rivals. Only UN sanctions imposed pursuant to Chapter VII of the UN Charter are legal. Unilateral sanctions contravene the letter and spirit of the UN Charter.

While arms embargoes are necessary and legitimate, because they aim to deescalate conflicts and give a chance to peace negotiations, economic sanctions aimed at "regime change" constitute a threat to the peace and stability of the world and should be condemned by the Security Council under article 39 of the Charter. Any country or group of countries can impose embargoes on the import and export of weapons by countries already at war or in danger of entering internal or external turmoil, but they should not gang-up on a geopolitical rival by imposing crippling economic sanctions and financial blockades that invariably impact the most vulnerable.

Experience shows that economic sanctions adversely impact the enjoyment of fundamental human rights by targeted popula-tions. Many sanctions, even "legal" sanctions imposed by the United Nations Security Council (e.g. against Iraq 1991–2003), can cause death, even massive death, as documented by UNICEF and other international organizations. It is estimated that at least 500,000 Iraqi children died because of these sanctions.[33] In Venezuela some 40,000 people died because of sanctions in 2018 alone.[34] Where it can be foreseen that sanctions will cause such havoc, they must be abolished and other methods must be tried that are consistent with the principles and purposes of the UN. Such sanctions also contravene international humanitarian

---

33 John Mulhall, "Sanctions 'have killed 500,000 Iraqi children,'" *Independent. ie,* July 22, 2000, https://www.independent.ie/world-news/sanctions-have-killed-500000-iraqi-children-26114461.html; "Razing the Truth About Sanctions Against Iraq," Geneva International Centre for Justice, https://www.gicj.org/positions-opinons/gicj-positions-and-opinions/1188-razing-the-truth-about-sanctions-against-iraq.

34 Mark Weisbrot and Jeffrey Sachs, "Economic Sanctions as Collective Punishment: The Case of Venezuela," Center for Economic and Policy Research, April 25, 2019, https://cepr.net/report/economic-sanctions-as-collective-punishment-the-case-of-venezuela/.

law, which specifically condemns "collective punishment." Moreover, sanctions regimes that disrupt or even asphyxiate the economies of the targeted countries result in widespread unemployment, hunger, disease, despair, emigration, and suicide. To the extent that such sanctions are "indiscriminate," they are tantamount to a form of "state terrorism," which by definition entails indiscriminate killing, similar to such repudiated weapons as land mines, cluster bombs and the use of cancer-producing depleted uranium weapons.[35]

It is a disgrace for the international community that the U.S. has flouted 29 General Assembly resolutions demanding the lifting of the illegal U.S. embargo against Cuba without facing some form of more explicit condemnation. It is a disgrace that notwithstanding General Assembly Resolution 76/161 of December 2021 and Human Rights Council Resolution 46/5 of March 2021—unequivocally condemning unilateral coercive measures and demanding their abolition—the United States, Canada, UK, and European Union have actually intensified economic sanctions affecting the rights of hundreds of millions of human beings the world over. To pretend that these sanctions have anything to do with promoting human rights is a *contradictio in adjecto*, an Orwellian cognitive dissonance.

The history of unilateral coercive measures is one of suffering and devastation. According to the theory, such sanctions are expected to "persuade" the targeted countries to change their policies. As the pundits like to predict, sanctions should lead to such public discontent that the population will arise in anger against their governments or lead to a coup d'état. Although the purpose of the sanctions is precisely to cause chaos, a national emergency, a volatile situation with unpredictable consequences, the political narrative that attempts to justify the sanctions invokes human rights and humanitarian principles as their true purpose. This is the classical instrumentalization of human rights for purposes of inducing "regime change." But are human

---

35 Catalinotto and Flounders (Eds.), *Depleted Uranium.*

rights served by the sanctions? Is there any empirical evidence showing that countries subjected to sanctions have improved their human rights records?

Experience shows that when a country is at war—any kind of war—it usually derogates from civil and political rights. Similarly, when a country is enduring non-conventional hybrid warfare and is subjected to economic sanctions and financial blockades, the result is *not* an expansion of human rights, but exactly the opposite. When sanctions trigger economic and social crises, governments routinely impose extraordinary measures and justify them because of the "national emergency." Accordingly, as in classical war situations, when a country is subject to a siege, it closes ranks in an attempt to regain stability through the temporary restriction of certain civil and political rights.

Article 4 of the International Covenant on Civil and Political Rights does envisage the possibility that governments may legitimately impose certain temporary restrictions, e.g. the derogation from Article 9 (detention), Article 14 (fair trial proceedings), Article 19 (freedom of expression), Article 21 (freedom of peaceful assembly), Article 25 (periodic elections). NO ONE wants such derogations, but every state's priority is survival, the defense of its sovereignty and identity. International law recognizes that governments have a certain margin of discretion in determining the level of threat to the survival of the state posed by sanctions, paramilitary activities, sabotage.

Thus, instead of facilitating the improvement of the human rights situation, economic sanctions often result in emergency domestic legislation that aims at safeguarding vital interests. In such cases sanctions reveal themselves as counter-productive, as a lose-lose proposition. Similarly, the overused practice of "naming and shaming" has revealed itself as ineffective. What has been effective in the past is quiet diplomacy, dialogue, and the willingness to compromise.

If the international community wants to help a country improve its human rights performance, it should endeavor to eliminate the threats that make governments retrench instead of opening-up. By now it should be obvious that sabre rattling, sanctions and blockades are not conducive to positive change. Precisely because they aggravate the situation and disrupt the proper functioning of state institutions, sanctions actually weaken the rule of law and lead to retrogression in human rights terms.

In the light of the continuing threats by some politicians against countries subjected to sanctions, it would seem that an old French adage has application—*la bête est très méchante, lorsqu'on l'attaque, elle se défend.* The beast is very nasty— when you attack it, it defends itself.

BOTTOM LINE

Let us recognize that "democracy" cannot be exported and imposed by force, that human rights are not the result of a vertical, top-down enforcement but rather require a horizontal recognition of the dignity of every human being, and that the exercise of human rights depends on education, mutual respect and solidarity.

It is imperative to reaffirm the reasons why unilateral coercive measures are incompatible with the object and purpose of the United Nations Charter and violate basic principles of the Charter including the sovereign equality of states, the self-determination of peoples, freedom of trade, freedom of navigation, non-discrimination, the obligation to solve differences by negotiation, the prohibition of the use of force.

A strong argument can be made that the language of article 2(4) of the Charter prohibiting "the threat or use of force" logically encompasses all forms of coercion against other states— coercion that would deny those countries the right to choose their form of government and their socio-economic system. Coercion cannot be used to impose a neoliberal economic system on other states. This is reflected in GA Resolutions 2131, 2625, 60/1 (para. 135), 76/161, OAS Charter Articles 19, 20, etc.[36]

It is imperative to reject the pretence that sanctions have anything to do with promotion of human rights. On the contrary—SANCTIONS KILL. Experience shows that sanctions are being used instead to advance geopolitical and geoeconomic agendas. The corporate media nonetheless continues to disseminate the propagandistic and profoundly erroneous argument that sanctions are imposed with the benevolent purpose of inducing countries to stop violating international law or stop violating human rights, and as such are morally preferable to outright military attack. Such is pure cynicism and hypocrisy.

Bearing in mind that the collateral impacts of economic sanctions and financial blockades result in the deaths of hundreds of thousands of innocent persons worldwide, it's time for the International Court of Justice to issue an advisory opinion enunciating point for point why such economic sanctions unilaterally imposed by states (as opposed to sanctions imposed by the Security Council, which are, in principle, legal, and sanctions against weapons sale and use) contravene international law. Such an advisory opinion should also define the legal consequences for the rogue states that impose sanctions, namely their obligation to lift them immediately and to make reparation to the targeted countries. Finally, the International Criminal Court must declare such sanctions to constitute crimes against humanity for purposes of article 7 of the Statute of Rome.

---

36 See in particular the Reports of the Special Rapporteurs of the Human Rights Council on the negative impacts of unilateral coercive measures, the late Dr. Idriss Jazairy and Professor Dr. Alena Douhan, "Special Rapporteur on unilateral coercive measures," UN Human Rights, Office of the High Commissioner: https://www.ohchr.org/EN/Issues/UCM/Pages/SRCoerciveMeasures.aspx. See also the language of the 29 General Assembly resolutions condemning the US embargo against Cuba.

13.

A Peoples' Tribunal for War Crimes

The idea of trying Vladimir Putin for war crimes is "trending" in social media, and some politicians like Joe Biden,[37] German President Frank-Walter Steinmeier,[38] and even some professors of international law are already concocting possible scenarios.

Without a doubt, the Russian invasion of Ukraine on 24 February 2022 entailed the crime of aggression for purposes of article 5 of the ICC statute and the 2010 Kampala definition of aggression. Had the invasion been in 1939 and had the aggressor been Germany, the case would have fallen within the scope of article 6(a) of the Nuremberg statute that defined the crime against peace.

The International Criminal Court in The Hague has, of course, a problem of jurisdiction, since neither Russia nor Ukraine are parties to the Statute of Rome of 1998.

What should the answer of the international community be to the war crimes already committed—on both sides—during this war? Both Russia and Ukraine are states parties to the Four Geneva Red Cross Conventions of 1949 and the 1977 Additional Protocols, which oblige them to investigate and prosecute members of their armed forces who are suspected of having committed grave breaches of international humanitarian law.

---

37 Cortney Drakeford, "Biden Demands Putin Face 'War Crime Trial' Amid Outrage Over Russia's Bucha Attack," *International Business Times,* April 4, 2022, https://www.ibtimes.com/biden-demands-putin-face-war-crime-trial-amid-outrage-over-russias-bucha-attack-3461268.

38 "German president calls for war crimes tribunal against Putin, Lavrov," *Reuters,* April 8, 2022, https://www.reuters.com/world/europe/german-president-calls-war-crimes-tribunal-against-putin-lavrov-spiegel-2022-04-08/; Gordon Brown, "Putin Must Face a War Crimes Tribunal for Ukraine Invasion," *Bloomberg,* March 9, 2022, https://www.bloomberg.com/opinion/articles/2022-03-10/putin-must-face-a-war-crimes-tribunal-for-ukraine-war.

This raises an additional issue concerning ICC jurisdiction. Indeed, to the extent that the State whose soldiers have committed war crimes undertakes to investigate and prosecute, the principle of complementarity excludes the admissibility of those cases by the ICC. Article 17 of the Rome Statute stipulates in part:

> the Court shall determine that a case is inadmissible where: (a) The case is being investigated or prosecuted by a State which has jurisdiction over it, unless the State is unwilling or unable genuinely to carry out the investigation or prosecution; (b) The case has been investigated by a State which has jurisdiction over it and the State has decided not to prosecute the person concerned, unless the decision resulted from the unwillingness or inability of the State genuinely to prosecute.

Accordingly, to the extent that the Russian and Ukrainian authorities carry out investigations in good faith and prosecute those found responsible for the alleged crimes, the ICC has no jurisdiction to pursue it.

Could the United Nations establish an *ad hoc* tribunal similar to the International Criminal Tribunal for the former Yugoslavia or the International Criminal Tribunal for Rwanda? The ICTY was established by UN Security Council Resolution 827 of May 25, 1993. The ICTR was established by UN Security Council Resolution 955 of November 8, 1994. By contrast, the UN Security Council would not be able to establish an ad hoc tribunal to try Putin, because both Russia and China would certainly exercise the veto power against it.

Thus, the frequent references to the Nuremberg Trials are mostly propagandistic. The historical conditions are not given in the context of the Ukraine war. Indeed, the 1945 International Military Tribunal was only possible because of Germany's unconditional surrender. There is zero chance of an unconditional surrender by Russia in the Ukraine war, and if NATO were to escalate further, we would be risking World War III and the Apocalypse of humanity. So, forget any victor's justice and *vae victis*, because there will only be vanquished.

Of course, the progressive development of international law has led to the expansion of the concept of universal jurisdiction, which enables any country to detain a person found within its territorial jurisdiction, if that person is suspected of having committed war crimes. Some countries like Germany and Sweden have already exercised universal jurisdiction over war crimes. Especially in cases of alleged genocide, a trial under universal jurisdiction would be conceivable if a given country can establish *in personam j*urisdiction against persons who are deemed to be *"hostes humani generis"*—enemies of all mankind. Yet another possibility would be to hold a trial *in absentia,* which would serve the purpose of documenting the crimes, even if the enforcement of the tribunal's judgment would be doubtful.

Those who are advocating a trial against Putin are in a typical liberal quandary—confronted by the binary scenario of clear criminality on one side and profound geopolitical hypocrisy on the other side. Professor Richard Falk writes wisely[39] that "Nuremberg did not establish a desirable legal precedent, because the drafters of the Nuremberg statute themselves betrayed fundamental principles of legality by applying criminal law selectively, since they overlooked their own criminality, having made no disposition to investigate the dropping of atom bombs on Hiroshima and Nagasaki" that together cost perhaps 250,000 civilian deaths (plus an additional hundred thousand for cancers, leukaemia and other medical sequels) or the carpet bombing of population centres in Germany, which resulted in some 600,000 charred corpses, e.g. in Dresden, Dortmund, Cologne, Berlin, Hamburg, Kassel—attacks that had little or no military significance and could only be described as pure terror. Falk is "far from sure about what is better from the perspective

---

39   Richard Falk, "Why Ukraine?" *CounterPunch,* April 8, 2022, https://www.counterpunch.org/2022/04/08/why-ukraine/.

of either developing a global rule of law or inducing respect for the restraints of law. The essence of law is to treat equals equally, but world order is not so constituted. As suggested, there is 'victors' justice' imposing accountability on the defeated leadership but complete non-accountability for the crimes of the geopolitical winners."

John LaForge,[40] co-director of Nukewatch, a peace and environmental justice group, proposes in his piece "Get in Line: Investigate U.S. Atrocities First" that a compilation of NATO crimes would be in order, including wars of aggression or occupation, the bombing of hospitals and schools, the desecration of corpses, attacks on civilians and civilian infrastructures, torturing and executing prisoners of war, using banned cluster bombs, etc.

> But unlike today's wall-to-wall news coverage of Russia's onslaught, the U.S. media mostly withdrew from reporting on U.S. military occupations and still chooses not to present many photos or film of alleged U.S. crimes. Like news censorship inside Russia, our media's blind eye helps maintain U.S. public support for its wars-of-choice, so protests have been raised mostly by victims, survivors, human rights groups, anti-war coalitions, and international law advocates.

LaForge's article lists some 200 atrocities for which the U.S. would be criminally responsible.

Personally, I would advocate convening "Peoples' Tribunals" with broad jurisdiction to investigate war crimes committed by all parties to the conflict. Surely the Ukrainians are compiling evidence of Russian crimes, as the Russians are compiling evidence of war crimes by Ukrainians and foreign mercenaries.

---

40 John LaForge, "Get In Line: Investigate U.S. Atrocities First," *CounterPunch*, April 8, 2022, https://www.counterpunch.org/2022/04/08/get-in-line-investigate-u-s-atrocities-first/.

Admittedly Peoples' Tribunals have no international recognition, and their judgments are not enforceable, but they do
have the added value of drawing attention to war crimes that
the mainstream media has ignored or even white-washed. A
Peoples' Tribunal would also collect the evidence, listen to the
testimony of hundreds of victims and identify the provisions of
the Geneva Conventions that have been violated.

I can refer to the Kuala Lumpur War Crimes Tribunal[41] that
sat in 2009–11 and convicted both George W. Bush and Tony
Blair of war crimes and crimes against humanity for the invasion
of Iraq in 2003, which the then UN Secretary General Kofi Annan
correctly described as an "illegal war."[42] The Kuala Lumpur
Tribunal sat again in 2013 to examine allegations of genocide
perpetrated by Israel against the Palestinians, and issued a judgment confirming the commission of the crime of genocide under
the 1948 Genocide Convention.[43]

The *Fondazione Lelio Basso* established the famous
Permanent Peoples' Tribunal,[44] which has held 49 sessions and
heard many cases since 1979, starting with the crimes committed by Morocco against the people of Western Sahara.[45]

Maybe a trial of Vladimir Putin, Volodymyr Zelinsky, Joe
Biden, Jens Stoltenberg and others would clarify many outstand-
ing legal and moral issues surrounding the war in Ukraine.

---

41 Richard Falk, "Kuala Lumpur tribunal: Bush and Blair guilty," *Aljazeera,*
November 28, 2011, https://www.aljazeera.com/opinions/2011/11/28/kuala-lumpur-
tribunal-bush-and-blair-guilty/.

42 "Iraq war illegal, says Annan," *BBC News,* September 16, 2004, http://news.
bbc.co.uk/1/hi/world/middle_east/3661134.stm.

43 "Judgment of the Kuala Lumpur Tribunal Re Israel War Crimes and
Genocide," *Covert Geopolitics,* February 16, 2020, https://geopolitics.co/2020/02/16/
judgment-of-the-kuala-lumpur-tribunal-re-israel-war-crimes-and-genocide/.

44 Permanent People's Tribunal (PPT): http://permanentpeoplestribunal.
org/?lang=en.

45 PPT Judgment: "01. Western Sahara (Brussels, 10-11 November 1979),"
http://permanentpeoplestribunal.org/sahara-occidentale-bruxelles-10-11-novembre-
1979/?lang=en.

DOUBLE STANDARDS

14.

Suspending Russia: A Precedent that Undermines the Credibility of the Human Rights Council

On April 7, 2022 the UN General Assembly decided to suspend Russia's membership in the Human Rights Council. This establishes a destructive precedent not only for the future of the Human Rights Council, but for the future of other United Nations institutions.

I do not wish to overestimate the consequences of the General Assembly decision. Obviously, it is a blow to Russia's prestige, and adds to the general atmosphere of Russophobia and growing hostility that we have seen over the decades.

We can expect in the future that efforts will be made to exclude other countries from membership in the Human Rights Council. Were such actions to be undertaken for due cause, excluding several NATO countries for the war crimes and crimes against humanity committed by their forces during the wars of aggression against Yugoslavia, Afghanistan, Iraq, Libya, Syria might be an option. We could think of excluding Saudi Arabia and the United Arab Emirates for their genocidal war against the people of Yemen. We could think of excluding India for its systematic war crimes and gross violations of human rights against the people of Kashmir, including widespread extra-judicial executions. Another credible candidate for suspension would be Azerbaijan because of its aggression against the hapless Armenians of Nagorno Karabakh during the *Blitzkrieg* of September–November 2020, where war crimes and crimes against humanity were committed, including torture and execution of Armenian prisoners of war. We could think of excluding Colombia because of its lethal para-military activities and consistent pattern of killing human rights defenders, social leaders, syndicalists and indigenous peoples. Of course, we could think of excluding the United States because of its multiple aggressions against so many countries, because of its support of terrorism, because of its "extraordinary rendition" program, because of systematic torture committed in Abu Ghraib, Mosul and Guantánamo. And so on.

Let us not shed too many tears over the Human Rights Council, whose authority and credibility are questionable, and whose resolutions are routinely ignored by many countries, including the United States, the United Kingdom and Israel. Since its creation in 2006 the Human Rights Council has not served human rights well—but it has certainly served the geopolitical and informational interests of the United States and the European Union.

The General Assembly decision also puts a further nail on the coffin of the General Assembly itself. It demonstrates how the Assembly can be and is manipulated by the United States and by the bullying, arm-twisting and blackmailing practices of the Department of State.

Far more serious for the world are the economic sanctions and financial blockade imposed by the U.S. and EU countries on Russia, which will have a long-lasting impact on the world economy, hurting the most vulnerable not only in Russia, but also in Europe, Africa, North and South America, and Asia. Nor will the U.S. itself be free of harm.

The decision of the General Assembly sets a dangerous precedent and further politicizes the Human Rights Council. One would think that precisely because some countries do not like what Russia is doing that they would like to "tame" it by involving it in the human rights work of the Council. Isolating a country is always counter-productive. What is needed is greater inclusion and greater debate—not exclusion and hate-mongering.

The General Assembly vote illustrates the success of the "information war" that has been waged against Russia for decades—not just since 2022, not even since 2014 and the Maidan coup—long before there was systematic disinformation about Russia and a consistent negative narrative. This has a simple explanation: NATO has had no *raison d'être* since the Warsaw Pact was dismantled in 1991. In order to continue to exist, NATO must have an "enemy"—and that is the only role that the U.S. and NATO envisage for Russia. The Russian bogeyman is necessary and guarantees that the U.S. military-industrial-financial complex can continue its war on the world and on the purposes and principles of the United Nations. There is zero interest on the part of NATO in promoting peaceful cooperation with Russia, cultural exchange, international understanding in the sense of the UNESCO Constitution. No matter how often Gorbachev and indeed Putin, sought friendship and integration with the West, it simply was not on NATO's agenda.

THE EVIDENCE BEFORE THE
GENERAL ASSEMBLY

The allegations of war crimes allegedly committed by Russian forces in Bucha in the vicinity of Kiev precipitated this move by the U.S. to have Russia removed from the Human Rights Council.

How much do we know about the events? While Ukraine accused Russia of murdering 400 civilians in Bucha before retreating from the town, the Russian government has refuted these allegations, pointing out that Russian forces withdrew in an orderly fashion on March 30 and that no allegations of extra judicial executions were made until April 2, four days later, when Ukrainian security forces and TV cameras arrived in Bucha.

The U.S. and NATO have accepted Kiev's claims uncritically and used them to justify imposing further sanctions against Russia. However, serious doubts have arisen about a possible staged event and tampering with the photos and videos. Do we have here another false flag operation, the like of which we have seen multiple times in Syria, such as staged chemical attacks that could not be confirmed by expert inspectors? Are the dead persons civilians or military? Were the bodies those of Russian soldiers and Ukrainian civilians, victims of artillery bombardment? Were the bodies wearing white armbands Russian soldiers or Ukrainian civilians with white armbands to signal their peaceful intentions, who were subsequently lynched by Ukrainian extremists for collaboration with the Russians? One day we may find out whether the U.S. had *post hoc* or even advance knowledge of the alleged crimes in Bucha or indeed, if it was involved in manufacturing evidence for the information war. Of course, nobody knows.

An international commission of inquiry should investigate, but that will take time, because the evidence on the ground (to the extent it has not been destroyed) must be evaluated and witnesses on all sides must be heard.

Gradually some information is coming out that does not confirm to Ukrainian claims: in a series of recorded satellite phone calls, a reporter identified as "Simon" tells his colleagues that at Borodyanka "there's no bodies in the streets at all," contrary to what he had been led to believe. Apparently, the town had been "shelled to pieces," but it is not clear whether by Russian or Ukrainian artillery. In any event, Simon concluded "there is no evidence of any rights abuses here." Simon and his crew interviewed residents who reported that the Russian soldiers had been correct and given them food, water and other supplies. Simon concluded: "I do not know what the prosecutor was talking about, but we have seen nothing like that. It is a completely different picture."

An international investigation is justified and necessary, but any *ad hoc* commission must investigate allegations of crimes committed not only by Russian soldiers but also by Ukrainian soldiers and paramilitaries, in particular, against the Russian

Ukrainians of Lugansk and Donetsk since 2014, and the earlier pogrom against 50 Russian Ukrainians carried out in Odessa in May 2014.

Therefore, it could be said without fear of contradiction, that the General Assembly vote was premature and violated general principles of law concerning due process and the presumption of innocence. According to the principle *"audiatur et altera pars"*—Russia's evidence and arguments must be heard and given due weight. The absence of due process is yet another disgrace for the General Assembly.

This is not the first and will not be the last time that the General Assembly applies double standards and adopts flawed resolutions or decisions. It seems like the entire United Nations system has been hijacked by the West and has the full support of a homologated corporate media that acts as echo chamber of the State Department.

DOUBLE STANDARDS AT THE
INTERNATIONAL CRIMINAL COURT

Another example of egregious double standards and selective indignation: The International Criminal Court. We hear politicians demand a "Nuremberg" Trial against Putin. Well, why not a Tribunal to investigate and condemn the crimes of aggression committed by Bill Clinton in Yugoslavia, by George W. Bush and Tony Blair in Iraq, by Barack Obama in Libya, Syria and Ukraine (after all, Obama was president when the "no fly" zone over Libya was manipulated for "regime change"—we all remember Hillary Clinton's infamous words: "We came, we saw, he died"[46]).

Any tribunal should also investigate the crimes committed by Ukrainian snipers at Maidan in connection with the 2014 *coup*

---

46 Hillary Clinton, "We Came, We Saw, He Died" (Gaddafi), YouTube video, 0:37, posted December 17, 2011 by NTCNATO, https://www.youtube.com/watch?v=FmIRYvJQeHM.

d'état against the democratically elected President of Ukraine, Viktor Yanukovych.

The International Criminal Court also has a responsibility to investigate and prosecute NATO forces from the U.S., UK, Germany, Australia, who committed atrocities e.g. in Afghanistan and Iraq? How about the torture centres in Iraq, Afghanistan and Guantánamo? How about the use of indiscriminate weapons, including depleted uranium weapons,[47] white phosphorus and cluster bombs, causing tens of thousands of deaths? How about all the "collateral damage" visited upon civilians in Afghanistan, Iraq, Syria and Libya?

Where is the accountability for all of these crimes?

The International Criminal Court will not have any credibility until it decides to apply the Statute of Rome seriously and go after the likes of George W. Bush, Tony Blair, Benjamin Netanyahu and Joe Biden. Hitherto, the West has "gotten away with it"—but for how long? Will the ICC remain in the service of the West, as a strong arm of the Pentagon? To date there appears to be a culture of impunity that protects Western leaders. Will the rule of law ever evolve into the rule of justice?

---

47 Catalinotto and Flounders (Eds.), *Depleted Uranium.*

15.

The UN Human Rights Council Hears What It Wants to Hear and Discards the Rest

It is no secret that the UN Human Rights Council essentially serves the interests of the Western developed countries and does not have a holistic approach to all human rights. Blackmail and bullying are common practices, and the U.S. has proven that it has sufficient "soft power" to cajole weaker countries into following its lead. It is not necessary to threaten in the chamber or in the corridors, a phone call from the Ambassador suffices. Countries are threatened with sanctions—or worse—as I have learned from African diplomats. Of course, if they abandon the illusion of sovereignty, they are rewarded by being called "democratic." Only major powers can afford to have their own opinions and to vote accordingly.

The UN Commission on Human Rights, which had been established by the General Assembly in 1946, was abolished in 2006. It was the Commission that had adopted the Universal Declaration of Human Rights in 1948 and numerous human rights treaties and created the system of UN Special Rapporteurs and thematic working groups.

At the time I was surprised by the rationale for the abolition given by the States members of the General Assembly, because the reason they put forward was the "politicization" of the Commission. Ironically, the U.S., one of the leading politicizers, was at the same time one of the principal critics of the Commission, unsuccessfully lobbying for the creation of a much smaller monitoring body, composed only of countries that observed human rights and therefore could pass judgment over the rest. Amazingly enough, the U.S. under George W. Bush presented itself as a "champion" of human rights.

Indeed, one might well question the merits of any process whereby such countries were to be determined. As it turned out, the General Assembly established a new body of 47 member States, the Human Rights Council, which, as any participant or observer will confirm today, is even more politicized and less objective than its maligned predecessor.

The special session of the HR Council held in Geneva on May 12, 2022 on the Ukraine war was a particularly painful event, marred by xenophobic statements in violation of article 20 of the International Covenant on Civil and Political Rights (ICCPR). Speakers employed a particularly mean tone to demonize Russia and Putin, while ignoring the war crimes committed by Ukraine, such as the 2014 Odessa massacre, the 8-year Ukrainian bombardment on the civilian population of Donetsk and Lugansk, etc.

A quick review of OSCE reports from February 2022 is revealing. The February 15 report of the OSCE Special Monitoring Mission to Ukraine recorded some 41 explosions in the ceasefire areas. This increased to 76 explosions on Feb. 16; 316 on Feb. 17; 654 on Feb. 18; 1413 on Feb. 19; a total of 2026 on Feb. 20 and 21; and 1484 on Feb. 22. The OSCE mission reports showed that the great majority of impact explosions of the artillery were on the separatist side of the ceasefire line.[48] We could easily make a comparison of the Ukrainian bombardment of the Donbas with Serbia's bombardment of Bosnia and Sarajevo in 1994 and 1995. But back then NATO's geopolitical agenda favored Bosnia and there, too, it divided the world into good guys and bad guys.

Any independent observer would cringe at the lack of balance displayed in the discussions at the Human Rights Council

---

48 See "OSCE Special Monitoring Mission to Ukraine (SMM) Daily Report 40/2022 issued on 21 February 2022," Organization for Security and Co-operation in Europe, https://www.osce.org/special-monitoring-mission-to-ukraine/512683.

on May 12, 2022. But are there many independent thinkers in the ranks of the "human rights industry" left? The pressure of conformism and "groupthink" is enormous. It has become "best practice" to gang up on Russia.

Notwithstanding the above considerations, the idea of establishing a commission of inquiry to investigate war crimes in Ukraine is not necessarily a bad one. But any such commission would have to be equipped with a broad mandate that would allow it to investigate war crimes by all belligerents—Russian soldiers as well as Ukrainian soldiers and the 20,000 mercenaries from 52 countries who are fighting on the Ukrainian side. According to Al-Jazeera, more than half of them, 53.7 percent, come from the United States, Britain and Canada, with 6.8 percent from Germany. Giving the commission a mandate to look into the activities of the 30 U.S./Ukrainian biolabs would also be justified.

What seems particularly offensive in the "spectacle" of May 12 at the Human Rights Council is that States engaged in rhetoric contrary to the human right to peace (GA Resolution 39/11) and to the right to life (art.6 ICCPR). The priority was not on saving lives by devising ways to promote dialogue and reach a sensible compromise that would usher an end to hostilities, but simply on condemning Russia and invoking international criminal law—of course, exclusively against Russia. Indeed, the speakers at the event engaged primarily in "naming and shaming," mostly evidence-free, since many of the allegations were not backed up by concrete facts worthy of a court of law. The accusers and the media also reiterated allegations that Russia had publicly addressed and refuted. What else is new? We already knew from the lyrics of the Simon & Garfunkel song, "The Boxer," that "a man hears what he wants to hear and disregards the rest."

Precisely the purpose of a commission of inquiry should be to collect verifiable evidence on all sides and to hear from as many witnesses as possible. This entails appointing independent experts from non-aligned countries as well as forensic experts to investigate the allegations of civilian killings, mass graves, extra-judicial executions, torture of prisoners of war, the activities of the U.S./Ukrainian biolabs, etc.

Unfortunately, the resolution adopted on May 12 does not augur well for peace and reconciliation, because it is woefully one-sided. For that very reason China departed from its practice of abstaining from such votes and voted against the resolution. It is laudable that the top Chinese diplomat at the UN Office in Geneva, Chen Xu, spoke about trying to mediate for peace and called for a global security architecture, deploring "that in recent years the politicization and confrontation at the [council] has been on the rise, which has severely impacted its credibility, impartiality and international solidarity." It is indeed bizarre and sad that it should be the "authoritarian" countries that are calling for more professionalism in the Council, while the "democracies" apparently only want to use the Human Rights Council to demonize others while advancing their geopolitical agendas, notwithstanding the human cost of prolonging the Ukraine war.

More important than the Geneva ritual exercise in Russia-bashing and the breathtaking hypocrisy of the resolution was another UN meeting, this time at the Security Council in New York, again on Thursday, May 12, where the Chinese deputy UN Ambassador Dai Bing argued that anti-Russia sanctions would certainly backfire, stating "Sanctions will not bring peace but will only accelerate the spill-over of the crisis, triggering sweeping food, energy and financial crises across the globe."

The next day at the Security Council, on Friday, May 13, Russia's Permanent Representative to the UN, Vassily Nebenzia, presented evidence documenting the dangerous activities of some 30 U.S. bio-laboratories in Ukraine.[49] He recalled the

---

49 "WATCH: UN Security Council on Ukraine's Bio Research," *Consortium News*, March 12, 2022, https://consortiumnews.com/2022/03/12/watch-un-security-council-on-ukraines-bio-research/; Patrick Howley, "Evidence Shows People Begging Ukraine President Zelensky To Close U.S. Biolab 'DEATH FACTORIES,'"

Biological and Toxin Weapons Convention of 1975 (BTWC) and expressed his preoccupation with the enormous risks involved in biological experiments carried out in U.S. warfare laboratories such as those at Fort Detrick, Maryland.

Nebenzia indicated that the Ukrainian biolabs were directly supervised by the U.S. Defense Threat Reduction Agency in the service of the Pentagon's National Center for Medical Intelligence. He confirmed the transfer abroad of more than 140 containers with ectoparasites of bats from a biolab in Kharkov, in the absence of any international control. Obviously, there is always an additional risk that pathogens may be stolen for terrorist purposes or sold in the black market. Evidence shows that dangerous experiments were conducted since 2014, following the Western-inspired and coordinated coup d'état against the democratically elected president of Ukraine, Victor Yanukovych.[50]

It appears that the U.S. program triggered a growing incidence of dangerous and economically relevant infections in Ukraine. Nebenzia stated "There is evidence that in Kharkov, where one of the labs is located, 20 Ukrainian soldiers died of swine flu in January 2016, 200 more were hospitalized. Besides, outbreaks of African swine fever occur regularly in Ukraine. In 2019 there was an outbreak of a disease that had symptoms similar to plague."

According to the Russian Ministry of Defense reports, the U.S. demanded that Kiev destroy the pathogens and cover up all traces of the research so that the Russian side would not get hold of the evidence of Ukrainian and U.S. violations of article 1 of the BTWC. Accordingly, Ukraine rushed to shut down all biological programs and Ukraine's health Ministry ordered the

---

National File, March 11, 2022, https://nationalfile.com/evidence-shows-people-begging-ukraine-president-zelensky-close-u-s-biolab-death-factories/.

50 Michael Welton, "Taking Aim at Ukraine: How John Mearsheimer and Stephen Cohen Challenged the Dominant Narrative," *CounterPunch,* May 5, 2022, https://www.counterpunch.org/2022/05/05/taking-aim-at-ukraine-how-john-mearsheimer-and-stephen-cohen-challenged-the-dominant-narrative/.

elimination of biological agents deposited in biolabs starting from February 24, 2022.

Ambassador Nebenzia pointed out that during a hearing in the U.S. Congress on March 8, Undersecretary of State Victoria Nuland confirmed that there were biolabs in Ukraine where military-purpose biological research had been conducted, and that it was imperative that these biological research facilities "should not fall in the hands of Russian forces."[51]

Meanwhile, the U.S. Ambassador to the UN, Linda Thomas-Greenfield, rejected the Russian evidence, calling it "propaganda" and gratuitously alluded to a discredited OPCW report on the alleged use of chemical weapons in Douma by President Bashar Al-Assad of Syria, thus seeking to discredit Russia by establishing a kind of guilt by association.

Even more pathetic was the statement delivered by UK Ambassador, Barbara Woodward, who called Russia's documented concerns "a series of wild, completely baseless and irresponsible conspiracy theories."

At that Security Council session, the Chinese Ambassador Dai Bing urged countries retaining weapons of mass destruction (WMDs), including biological and chemical weapons, to destroy their stockpiles: "We firmly oppose the development, stockpiling and use of biological and chemical weapons by any country under any circumstances, and urge countries that have not yet destroyed their stockpiles of biological and chemical weapons to do so as soon as possible. Any information trail of bio-military activity should be of great concern to the international community." China called on all concerned parties to respond to relevant questions in a timely manner and make comprehensive clarifications so as to dispel the legitimate doubts of the international community.

---

51 "Victoria Nuland admits to the existence of US biolabs in Ukraine 03.08.22," video posted March 9, 2022 on *Gab TV,* https://sage.gab.com/channel/trump_won_2020_twice/view/victoria-nuland-admits-to-the-existence-62284360aaee086c4bb8a628.

I forecasted that the mainstream media would give abundant visibility to the U.S. and UK statements and blithely ignore the evidence presented by Russia and China's proposals—as indeed, it did.

There is more bad news for peace and sustainable development. Bad news for disarmament, in particular nuclear disarmament; bad news on the ever increasing military budgets and the waste of resources for the arms race and war. As it concerns Finland's and Sweden's bid to join NATO: do they realize that they are potentially joining an organization that could be considered a "criminal organization" for purposes of article 9 of the statute of the Nuremberg Tribunal? Are they conscious of the fact that over the past 30 years NATO has committed the crime of aggression and war crimes in Yugoslavia, Afghanistan, Iraq, Libya and Syria, including the use of indiscriminate weapons and depleted uranium weapons that have significantly polluted the victim countries and increased the incidence in cancers and leukaemia?[52] Of course, NATO has thus far enjoyed impunity. But "getting away with it" does not render such crimes any less criminal.

While the credibility of the Human Rights Council is not yet dead, we must admit that it is seriously wounded. Alas, the Security Council does not earn any laurels either. Both are gladiator arenas where countries are mainly trying to score points. Will these two institutions ever develop into civilized fora of constructive debate over matters of war and peace, life and death, human dignity and the very survival of humanity?

---

52 Catalinotto and Flounders (Eds.), *Depleted Uranium.*

16.

Precedents of Permissibility

Russia's aggression against Ukraine entails a grave violation of the *jus cogens* rule stipulated in article 2, paragraph 4, of the UN Charter—the prohibition of the use of force without approval of the Security Council. Admittedly, Russia has invoked article 51 of the Charter, which recognizes the right of self-defense until the Security Council is seized of the matter. However, this provision only operates when there has been a prior military attack, which a state must repulse, because its very survival is at stake. This is not the case in the current conflict.

It is deplorable that some legal experts have evoked the idea of pre-emptive self-defense to justify the invasion. There is no right to "preemptive self-defense" in treaty law as there is none in customary international law. The "principle" is as invalid here as it was when George W. Bush invoked it to justify his war of aggression on Iraq in 2003.

Some observers have suggested a justification based on the concept of vital interests of the state, which Israel invokes from time to time in an attempt to justify its crimes against Palestinians, Lebanese, Syrians and others. Only apologists would buy these arguments that lack any legitimacy in international law—or natural law.

Our priority today must be to work for an immediate cease fire, followed by urgent humanitarian assistance and a truly international conference that would attempt to reach a compromise that would be conducive to durable peace in the region. A compromise means just that: there must be give and take. The Cuban missile crisis of 1962 was resolved through a pragmatic quid pro quo, whereby the Soviets pulled their missiles out of Cuba, and the United States removed its missiles from Turkey.

Such an international peace conference would have to over-
come the propaganda and "fake news" that have plagued the
conflict since well before the outbreak of hostilities. The conference would have to base its deliberations on empirical evidence
and discard the skewed narratives that render it practically
impossible to address the issues in a realistic manner. Assuming
that there is good faith on all sides, the conference should
pursue its peace-making function relying on evidence-based,
rational argumentation, solidly anchored in a comprehensive
evaluation of all pertinent factors, including the pre-history of
the conflict, breaches of oral agreements, mutual perceptions of
bad faith, the interference in the internal affairs of states, the
instrumentalization and foreign financing of non-governmental
organizations as trojan horses to destabilize governments, the
unconstitutional coup d'état against the democratically elected
President of Ukraine, Viktor Yanunovych, the denial of the right
of internal self-determination to ethnic Russians and Russian
mother tongue Ukrainians, the Russophobic legislation of the
Ukrainian Parliament, the violence practiced against the Donbas
Russians, the flouting of the agreements of Minsk 1 and Minsk 2,
the constant provocations and threats in violation of article 2(4)
of the UN Charter, which prohibits not only the use of force, but
also the threat thereof.

Notwithstanding the bogus narratives we read in the corporate press, this conflict did not emerge out of the blue, but was
the result of cumulative errors and abuses and of an atmosphere
of deception, hostility and "hate speech."

The current political constellation and the toxic atmosphere
that has been generated against anything Russian constitute
major obstacles to constructive solutions. As pre-conditions to
any successful negotiation one would expect the capacity of
all parties to take a certain distance, demonstrate a measure of
mutual respect and an honest effort at approaching the conflict
from different perspectives.

Groupthink jumps to the eye when one observes the way
in which the mainstream media reports on the conflict and the

almost total absence of balance, the invisibility of the arguments of the other side, which have been formulated over the years and have been ignored by Western politicians and journalists. Only a few academics like Professors John Mearsheimer, Francis Boyle, Dan Kovalik, Noam Chomsky, only certain diplomats like Jack Matlock and George F. Kennan seem to have understood what was at issue: the right of every country to national security and the necessity to build a durable European—and world—security architecture.

The two proposals put forward by Russia in December 2021 would have deserved serious consideration and general debate—instead of being arrogantly put aside by the U.S. and NATO. The rejection of these proposals and the refusal of Ukraine to implement the Minsk Agreements of 2014 and 2015 to which it had previously agreed has led directly to today's tragedy. As addressed in the previous chapter, the OSCE mission reports showed a striking increase in the number of explosions on the separatist side of the ceasefire line in the period immediately preceding the Russian Special Military Operation.[53] We could easily make a comparison of the Ukrainian bombardment of the Donbas with Serbia's bombardment of Bosnia and Sarajevo in 1994 and '95. But back then, NATO's geopolitical agenda favored Bosnia and there, too, it divided the world into good guys and bad guys.

On February 19 Ukrainian President Zelensky announced at the Munich Security Conference that the Ukraine would ditch the Budapest memorandum and all related agreements. The Budapest memorandum is about Ukraine committing to be a non-nuclear state.[54]

---

53 Organization for Security and Co-operation in Europe, "OSCE Special Monitoring Mission to Ukraine (SMM) Daily Report 40/2022 issued on 21 February 2022," *OSCE,* https://www.osce.org/special-monitoring-mission-to-ukraine/512683.

54 Zelensky's full speech at Munich Security Conference," *The Kyiv Independent,* February 19, 2022, https://kyivindependent.com/national/zelenskys-full-speech-at-munich-security-conference/; Avis Krane, "Zelensky's statement. A bluff or a dream of nuclear weapons?" *Essence of Time,* February 21, 2022, http://eu.eot.su/2022/02/21/zelenskys-statement-a-bluff-or-a-dream-of-nuclear-weapons/

In November–December 2021 and January–February 2022 we witnessed Russia's concerted efforts to reach a modus vivendi with the West and an exponential increase in the number of provocations by the Ukraine and NATO. An objective third

Map of recorded ceasefire violations

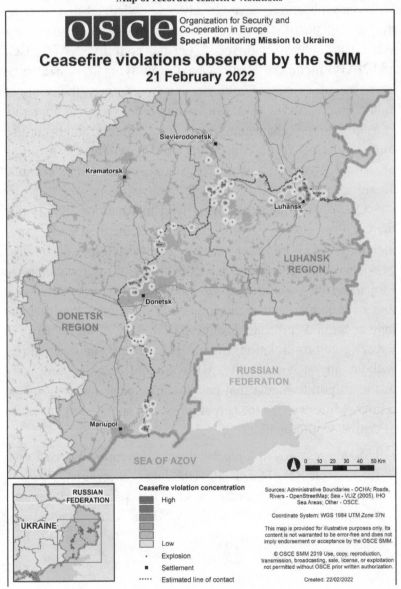

party should have no difficulty in understanding Russia's concerns and would not have simply and perfunctorily repeated the State Department and Pentagon narratives. There is no doubt that assurances were given to Soviet leaders that NATO would not expand eastward. In fact, there is no reason for the existence of NATO, once the Warsaw Pact was dismantled.

Many observers have already acknowledged that, judging by NATO's post-Cold War practices, it can in no sense be considered a "defensive alliance." On the contrary. NATO itself and NATO members have engaged in bullying and threatening other countries. NATO countries have committed the crime of aggression, as well as war crimes and crimes against humanity in Yugoslavia, Afghanistan, Iraq, Libya, Somalia, and Syria—in total impunity. Would this bring NATO within the meaning of article 9 of the Nuremberg Statute concerning "criminal organizations"?

One of the major problems with international law is that there is no effective enforcement mechanism. (And here I include the R2P initiative which was distorted and discredited by serving to implement the West's policy of regime change in Libya.) Serial violations of the UN Charter have resulted in a loss of authority and credibility—and the emergence of what may be termed "precedents of permissibility." A non-exhaustive list of egregious violations of the UN Charter by many countries without any accountability, with the unfortunate complicity of the corporate media that has downplayed the gravity of the crimes, white-washed the perpetrators, and suppressed the views of critics, would include:

• U.S. aggressions and regime-change attempts against Cuba, Dominican Republic, Haiti, Honduras, Nicaragua, Panama, Venezuela, the "extraordinary rendition" program, systematic torture and indefinite detention in Guantánamo Naval Base, targeted assassinations

- Israel's multiple aggressions against its Arab neighbours, the occupation and annexation of Palestinian territories, East Jerusalem, the Golan Heights, Israel's continued bombardment of Syria, targeted assassination, the use of cluster-bombs and other illegal weapons in the war against Lebanon, etc.

- Turkey's invasion and bombardment of Cyprus in 1974, the killing of thousands of Greek-Cypriots and the expulsion of some 200,000 Greek Cypriots from Northern Cyprus to the South, the continued occupation of 37% of the territory of the island, the refusal to implement judgments of the European Court of Human Rights.

- Saudi Arabia and the UAE's murderous war against the Yemeni people, its illegal blockade and responsibility for the bombardment of schools, the killing of tens of thousands of civilians, and the starving of the population, resulting in the world's greatest humanitarian crisis.

- Azerbaijan's aggression, together with Turkey and Libyan and Syrian mercenaries in the September 2020 Blitzkrieg against the Armenians of Nagorno Karabakh, entailing thousands of civilian deaths, the destruction of churches and monasteries and the violation of the right of self-determination to the Armenian people.

- Turkey's repeated bombardments of Kurdish villages and refugee camps in Iraq, particularly in 2021 and more recently in 2022, in the midst of the Ukraine war.[55]

It is a disgrace that the international community tolerated these crimes of aggression, war crimes and crimes against

---

55 "Turkish air strike kills at least three in refugee camp in Iraq," *Reuters,* June 5, 2021; https://www.reuters.com/world/middle-east/turkish-air-strike-kills-least-three-refugee-camp-inside-iraq-2021-06-05/; "Turkey strikes PKK targets in Iraq's Kurdistan region," *Al-Monitor,* August 24, 2021, https://www.al-monitor.com/originals/2021/08/turkey-strikes-pkk-targets-iraqs-kurdistan-region; Jared Szuba, "Turkey steps up attacks on Syria's Kurds amid Iraq operation," *Al-Monitor,* April 22, 2022, https://www.al-monitor.com/originals/2022/04/turkey-steps-attacks-syrias-kurds-amid-iraq-operation.

humanity without demanding accountability from the perpetrators. This is what I refer to when I speak of "precedents of
permissibility."

Indeed, if NATO countries, Israel, Azerbaijan, Saudi Arabia
and other states commit crimes in total impunity, does not this
encourage other states to do the same? Double standards in the
application of international law and international criminal law
undermine the entire system.

That is precisely what Friedrich von Schiller meant in his
drama *Piccolomini*: *Das eben ist der Fluch der bösen Tat, dass
sie fortzeugend immer Böses muss gebären.* That is: the curse of
an evil deed is that it continues generating further evils.

Lessons learned: the multiple violations of the prohibition
of the use of force by powerful States without Security Council
approval—and this in total impunity—cannot and did not change
international law nor could it derogate from article 2(4) of the
UN Charter. The general principle of law *ex injuria non oritur
jus*—"out of a violation of law, no new law can emerge"—
prevents the recognition of a new norm allowing aggression.
However, such repeated violations have given rise to "precedents
of permissibility," because in reality countries do get away with
criminal activity, because the UN lacks appropriate enforcement mechanisms. The International Criminal Court possesses
little authority and credibility and is hardly a deterrent force,
because hitherto it has only indicted Africans and it has refused
to investigate some of the most egregious aggressions and war
crimes committed since the Statute of Rome entered into force
in 2002. Today the aggressor may be Russia, but over the past
20 years we have seen aggressions and war crimes committed
by NATO countries, notably the U.S., UK, France, Germany,
Turkey, Australia, and by other countries such as Saudi Arabia,
Azerbaijan, India, China, Myanmar, etc. Yes, the ICC should
investigate war crimes committed in the Ukrainian war, but it
must also investigate and condemn prior crimes if it wants to be
taken seriously. If international law is to have credibility, it must
be applied uniformly.

17.

The Unsung Indigenous Victims of North and South America

On the 12th of October many celebrate the "discovery" of what became known as America by Christopher Columbus. What do we learn in history books about the colonization of North and South America? Indeed, what do we understand under the term "History"? What uses does the writing of history have? As Herodotus noted, history-writing means "inquiry," a vocation further developed and applied by Thucydides.

Ideally, history should be a contextual timeline of true events, reflecting the seven "Cs" of historical analysis—chronology, context, coherence, comprehensiveness, causality, comparison and *cui bono* (who stands to gain from an event and from a particular narrative). Yet, as can be easily demonstrated, historians throughout the ages have manipulated the record—primarily by omitting crucial facts, sometimes by inventing them, a phenomenon attributable to opportunism, career expectations, political correctness, literary enthusiasm, poetic license (*se non è vero è molto ben trovato!*), optimism (feel good stories), and sometimes greed.

Let's face it, many historians—like lawyers—write for a specific audience. The name of the game is not necessarily uncovering the truth; frequently it is catering to a client or a specific reading public. Both lawyers and historians write what they believe is expected of them, or what will render to them social and economic benefits. This is why historical accounts that raise uncomfortable questions and upset the established order, i.e. are not black and white, neatly separating good and bad, heroes and villains, are seldom written, and if written, are difficult to place with commercial publishers, and thus marginalized, are often ignored by the corporate media and by other accommodated pens for hire. Since my historical studies at the Harvard Graduate School of Arts and Sciences and following my historical dissertation and doctorate at the University of Göttingen in Germany in 1977, I have had multiple experiences with the professional associations of historians in several countries. My impression is that the ethos of scholarship is low and that many historians write with a pre-conceived idea and regularly suppress information that does not fit the matrix. Lawyers and UN "rapporteurs" often do the same.

Let us now revisit a major historical event that is mostly perceived in the U.S. and Europe as a success story—the European colonization of North and South America—where the genocides that entailed are still widely unrecognized by the general public, despite noteworthy scholarly works on the subject.[56]

Now, did the Europeans really "discover" an empty continent, which they then settled and developed, or were our ancestors more like "migrants" to new frontiers? Let us look at

---

56 Bartolomé de las Casas, *Brief History of the Devastation of the Indies* (Baltimore, Md.: Johns Hopkins Univ. Press, 1992); Daniel Castro, *Another Face of Empire: Bartolomé de Las Casas, Indigenous Rights, and Ecclesiastical Imperialism* (Durham, NC: Duke Univ. Press, 2007); David Stannard, *American Holocaust* (Oxford, England: Oxford Univ. Press, 1992); Richard Drinnon, *Facing West* (Norman, Okla.: Univ. of Oklahoma Press, 1997); Frederick E. Hoxie (ed.), *Encyclopedia of North American Indians* (Collingdale, Pa.: Diane Publishing Co., 1999), in particular see Russell Thornton, "Population: Precontact to Present," 500–502; Carl Waldman and Molly Braun, *Atlas of the North American Indian* (New York: Facts on File, 1985); Francis Jennings, *The Invasion of America* (Chapel Hill, NC: Univ. of North Carolina Press, 1975); Nicholas Guyatt, *Providence and the Invention of the United States* (Cambridge: Cambridge Univ. Press, 2007); Richard Warner van Alstyne, *The Rising American Empire* (Oxford, England: Oxford Univ. Press, 1960); Reginald Horsman, *Expansion and American Indian Policy 1983–1812* (East Lansing, Mich.: Michigan State University Press, 1967); Noam Chomsky, *Hopes and Prospects* (New York: Penguin, 2010), 16–24; Ward Churchill, *Struggle for the Land: Native North American Resistance to Genocide, Ecocide and Colonization* (San Francisco: City Lights Books, 2002); Alexander Laban Hinton, Andrew Woolford, Jeff Benvenuto, *Colonial Genocide in Indigenous North America* (Durham, NC: Duke Univ. Press, 2014); Tamara Starblanket, *Suffer Little Children,* (Atlanta, Ga.: Clarity Press, 2019).

Europe during the "age of discovery." Our European ancestors were relatively poor, our cities were squalid and overcrowded; unemployment, disease and violence were rife. The 16th, 17th, 18th, 19th and even 20th century migrants—the Spanish, the Portuguese, the British, the French. the Dutch, the Germans, the Poles, the Irish, the Ukrainians and many other migrants—were initially religious refugees, adventurers, mavericks bent on getting rich fast, followed by simple folk hoping for a new start. The historical fact is that what we know today as North America (the Western hemisphere north of the Rio Grande) was a rich land, ecologically-balanced, populated by some 10 million human beings, minding their own business and posing no threat to Europeans, when in 1492 Christopher Columbus landed on Guanahani, an Island in the Bahamas, thinking that he had found a western route to India. Columbus went on to Cuba and the Antilles, undertook four voyages to the Americas, still thinking that the inhabitants were "Indians."

Unlike the Spaniards, who "Christianised" the indigenous populations and used them as cheap labour, our Anglo-Saxon forebears had little use for the natives, whom they referred to as "devils" and "wolves." The Massachusetts Puritans, who also burned witches, killed the native "Indians" who had taught them how to survive, while the Reverend John Cotton of the first Church of Boston, and the Reverend Cotton Mather of the Second Church of Boston held their racist, rabble-rousing sermons worthy of a Julius Streicher. In the course of three centuries 98% of the native North American population was not only displaced pursuant to the official policy of "manifest destiny" but it also fell victim to European diseases, dislocation, destruction of their economic base, deliberate burning of their crops and continuous massacres since the early days of the Massachusetts colony.

The founding fathers of the "land of the free and the home of the brave"—Benjamin Franklin ("the design of Providence to extirpate these savages"), George Washington ("beasts of prey"), John Adams ("blood hounds"), Thomas Jefferson ("merciless Indian savages"), James Madison, James Monroe, Andrew Jackson ("the wolf be struck in his den")—all called for the extinction of the American "Indian." In 1803 President Thomas Jefferson delivered a Confidential Message to Congress on Indian Policy explaining a strategy to dispossess Indian Tribes of their territories in part by assimilation, in part by taking advantage of their naiveté and driving them into debt so as to more easily strip them of their lands.[57]

There is damning evidence that Lord Jeffrey Amherst had genocidal intent ("... that Vermine ... have forfeited all claim to the rights of humanity) and actually waged germ warfare on the Indigenous by deliberately delivering smallpox-contaminated blankets.[58] These dreadful historical facts, having long slept in the archives, are slowly coming to light, if anyone cares to consult them. But most American historians and the mainstream media only choose to remember "Thanksgiving Day" and the story of Pocahontas.

MESO-AND SOUTH AMERICA

What we know as Meso- and South America was also a rich land, densely populated with some 70 million human beings, with magnificent cities like Tenochtitlan (today Mexico City), capital of the Aztec kingdom, with towns, villages, impressive architecture, aqueducts, sports facilities, science, astronomy, and art.

---

57 Rebecca Cohen, "Thomas Jefferson once secretly wrote to Congress that the US would try to drive Native Americans into debt in order to take their land," *Yahoo! News,* May 12, 2022, https://news.yahoo.com/thomas-jefferson-once-secretly-wrote-152313663.html; Bryan Newland, *Federal Indian Boarding School Initiative Investigative Report,* Bureau of Indian Affairs, U.S. Department of the Interior, May 2022, https://www.bia.gov/sites/default/files/dup/inline-files/bsi_investigative_report_may_2022_508.pdf

58 Carl Waldman and Molly Braun (illustrator), *Atlas of the North American Indian* (New York: Facts on File, 1985); Peter D'Errico, "Jeffery Amherst and Smallpox Blankets," University of Massachusetts Amherst, https://people.umass.edu/derrico/amherst/lord_jeff.html.

Their vast agricultural lands produced such wonderful foods as avocados (*ahuacatl* in Aztec, originating in the Tehuacán valley near Oaxaca), beans, blueberry, cacao, cashews, cassava, cayenne pepper, chilli peppers, gourds, jalapeños, maize (*mahiz* in Arawak language, commonly known as corn), passion fruit, peanuts, pecans, pineapple, quinine (tonic water!), sunflowers (*helianthus*), sweet pimentos, potatoes (*papa* or *patata* in Inca language), pumpkin, squash, tapioca, tomatoes (*tomatl* in Nahuatl language), topinanbour, vanilla, zucchini, etc., not to mention that very bad import to Europe—tobacco (from the Arawakan or Taino word referred to by the Dominican friar, later Bishop Bartolomé de Las Casas), hitherto unknown in Europe (until introduced in Spain in 1558 by Francisco Fernandez).[59]

As we can read in the writings of Las Casas, our Spanish ancestors brutally aggressed against the indigenous population, murdered and enslaved millions of the men, raped their women, and eventually mixed with the survivors to create the "mestizo" society we know in Latin America today. If you travel to Mexico, Guatemala, El Salvador, Honduras, Nicaragua, Colombia, Venezuela, Ecuador, Peru, Bolivia, Paraguay—you will see the descendants of the Aztecs, the Mayas, the Incas, the Quechuas, the Guaranis. So much for the "discovery" of the Americas and for the legal fiction of *"terra nullius."*

It is worth remembering that, far from being xenophobic, the first nations of the Americas received Cristóbal Colón with remarkable hospitality, as Columbus himself acknowledged in his writings. The European newcomers, however, were migrants with the sword. Perhaps the only good thing that can be said for Spanish colonization is that the human rights activities of Friar Antonio de Montesinos ("Are these not also men"?) and Bartolomé de las Casas before Emperor Charles V led to the

---

59 Other foods are native to North America including cranberry (native to the region around Edmonton, Alberta, in Canada), maple sugar and maple syrup (produced by the Ojibwe and Algonquin peoples of Northeast Canada), "wild rice" (anishinaabe manoomin, hand-harvested by Anishinaabe peoples in central-north America).

adoption of the "New Laws" of 1542 which recognized the human nature of the indigenous population and forbade their ill-treatment and enslavement.

The great disputations of Valladolid 1550–51 have gone down in history as a milestone in the development of the concept of human rights. Admittedly, Charles' laws were violated with impunity, which only illustrates the truism that norms and their enforcement are not identical. Yet, if we had no norms, we would be totally subject to the law of the jungle, otherwise known as "might makes right." Unfortunately, the Popes were more like corporate executives or "managers" and showed little interest in the humanity of the natives, supporting instead the ambitions and the greed of the Spanish and Portuguese rulers with the infamous Papal bulls *Inter Caetera*[60] and *Dudum Siquidem,*[61] both of 1493, laying the foundation for the unethical doctrine of "discovery"[62] which has yet to be repudiated despite recent requests by natives in Canada, pursuant to the Pope's "Apology" for the Church's role in the abuse of native children in Canada's residential schools.[63]

WHAT INDIGENOUS NAMES IN AMERICA TELL US

Now that it has become "politically correct" to condemn the discrimination and humiliation of Afro-Americans, will historians and the media finally come to grips with the discrimination, exclusion and aggressions against the First Nations of the Americas? When will the mainstream media recognize

---

60 Pope Alexander VI, "Division of the undiscovered world between Spain and Portugal" (1493), *Papal Encyclicals Online,* https://www.papalencyclicals.net/Alex06/alex06inter.htm.

61 Johannes Nilis and P. Gormaz, "The Bull Dudum Siquidem of September 26, 1493," *The Reformation Online,* https://www.reformation.org/dudum-siquidem.html.

62 *Doctrine of Discovery,* https://doctrineofdiscovery.org/papal-bulls/.

63 Michael Swan, "Indigenous demand Pope Francis revoke Doctrine of Discovery," *The Catholic Register,* March 31, 2022, https://www.catholicregister.org/home/international/item/34212-indigenous-demand-pope-francis-revoke-doctrine-of-discovery.

the crimes committed against the indigenous, the hundreds of broken treaties, including the treaty of Laramie of 1864 that had recognized the Black Hills of South Dakota as Sioux property in perpetuity, and discarded as soon as gold was found there. There, too, was the massacre of Wounded Knee—where there, too, were the Four Heads of white American Presidents sculpted on the sacred hills of Mount Rushmore, two of whom were slave owners and all four of whom were "Indian" haters.[64]

We all now agree that the endemic racism against Afro-Americans is criminal, their reduction to slavery, their century-long segregation, lynchings by the Ku Klux Klan and others.[65] By contrast, four centuries of massacres and exploitation of the Algonquins, Cherokees, Crees, Iroquois, Mohawks, Navajos, Pequots, Seminoles, Sioux have not elicited comparable general outrage or even interest in the public or in the mainstream media. There is no apology or remorse for their ongoing discrimination.

The clash of civilizations during the 16th–20th centuries, when European migrants destroyed the livelihoods of 70–80 million North and South American Indigenous is ongoing. And yet, the physical and cultural genocide perpetrated against the First Nations of the Americas curiously remains an under-reported, relatively taboo subject, except for a few scholarly books by Professors David Stannard, Richard Drinnen, and the 2014 anthology *Colonial genocide in Indigenous North America,* edited by Alexander Laban Hinton, Andrew Woolford, Jeff Benvenuto.

64 "The Six Grandfathers Before It Was Known as Mount Rushmore," *Native Hope,* https://blog.nativehope.org/six-grandfathers-before-it-was-known-as-mount-rushmore (accessed May 25, 2022); Alysa Landry, "Theodore Roosevelt: 'The Only Good Indians Are the Dead Indian," June 28, 2016 (updated September 13, 2018), https://indiancountrytoday.com/archive/theodore-roosevelt-the-only-good-indians-are-the-dead-indians-oN1cdfuEW02KzOVVyrp7ig; "Sacré mont Rushmore," *Le Courrier de Genève* August 2, 2012; Ron Way, "The real history of Mount Rushmore," *StarTribune,* July 29, 2016, https://www.startribune.com/the-real-history-of-mount-rushmore/388715411/.

65 NAACP, "History of Lynching in America," https://naacp.org/find-resources/history-explained/history-lynching-america.

INDIAN LAND FOR SALE

GET A HOME
OF
YOUR OWN

EASY PAYMENTS

PERFECT TITLE

POSSESSION
WITHIN
THIRTY DAYS

wikipedia · www.CALIE.ORG

FINE LANDS IN THE WEST

IRRIGATED IRRIGABLE **GRAZING** **AGRICULTURAL DRY FARMING**

IN 1910 THE DEPARTMENT OF THE INTERIOR SOLD UNDER SEALED BIDS ALLOTTED INDIAN LAND AS FOLLOWS:

Location	Acres	Average Price per Acre	Location	Acres	Average Price per Acre
Colorado	5,211.21	$7.27	Oklahoma	34,664.00	$19.14
Idaho	17,013.00	24.85	Oregon	1,020.00	15.43
Kansas	1,684.50	33.45	South Dakota	120,445.00	16.53
Montana	11,034.00	9.86	Washington	4,879.00	41.37
Nebraska	5,641.00	36.65	Wisconsin	1,069.00	17.00
North Dakota	22,610.70	9.93	Wyoming	865.00	20.64

FOR THE YEAR 1911 IT IS ESTIMATED THAT **350,000** ACRES WILL BE OFFERED FOR SALE

For information as to the character of the land write for booklet, "INDIAN LANDS FOR SALE," to the Superintendent U. S. Indian School at any one of the following places:

CALIFORNIA: Hoopa. **COLORADO:** Ignacio. **IDAHO:** Lapwai. **KANSAS:** Horton. Nadeau. **MINNESOTA:** Onigum. **MONTANA:** Crow Agency. **NEBRASKA:** Macy. Santee. Winnebago. **NORTH DAKOTA:** Fort Totten. Fort Yates. **OKLAHOMA:** Anadarko. Cantonment. Colony. Darlington. Muskogee. Pawnee. **OKLAHOMA—Con.** Sac and Fox Agency. Shawnee. Wyandotte. **OREGON:** Klamath Agency. Pendleton. Roseburg. Siletz. **SOUTH DAKOTA:** Cheyenne Agency. Crow Creek. Greenwood. Lower Brule. Pine Ridge. Rosebud. Sisseton. **WASHINGTON:** Fort Simcoe. Fort Spokane. Tekoa. Tulalip. **WISCONSIN:** Oneida.

WALTER L. FISHER, Secretary of the Interior.

ROBERT G. VALENTINE, Commissioner of Indian Affairs.

If people are pulling down monuments of U.S. Confederate officers, will they also pull down statues of the killers of native Americans, including President Andrew Jackson, General William Sherman, and General Philip Sheridan, who coined the phrase "The only good Indian is a dead Indian"?

Let us pause and reflect on what indigenous place names in the U.S. and Canada tell us:

Back in 1970 I hitchhiked across the United States and observed that there were literally tens of thousands of indigenous names from the Atlantic to the Pacific. Names like: Adirondack, Alabama, Alaska, Algonquin, Allegheny, Apache, Apalachee, Appalachia, Appomattox, Arkansas, Biloxi, Calumet, Calusa, Canada, Caribou, Cayuga, Chatanooga, Chautauqua, Chepanoc, Cherokee, Chesapeake, Cheyenne, Chicago, Chickasaw, Chilliwak, Chinook, Chipola, Chippewa, Chiwawa, Choctaw, Clatsop, Coloma, Colusa, Comanche, Commack, Connecticut, Coquitlam, Cree, Curyung, Cuyahoga, Dakota, Delaware, Denali, Detroit, Erie, Hackensack, Hawaii, Hialeah, Hiawatha, Hopi, Huron, Idaho, Illinois, Inola, Inyo, Iowa, Iroquois, Kalamazoo, Kanab, Kansas, Kelowna, Kenosha, Kentucky, Keweenaw, Klondike, Kuskokwim, Lillooet, Mackinac, Mackinaw, Malibu, Maliseet, Manatee, Manhattan, Manitoba, Mantou, Mattawa, Massachusetts, Meramec, Merrick, Merrimac, Metoac, Miami, Miccosukee, Michigan, Michipicuten, Micmac, Milwaukee, Minnesota, Minnewanka, Mississippi, Missouri, Moab, Moccasin, Modoc, Mohawk, Mohegan, Mohican, Mojave, Monache, Montauk, Muscogee, Muskegan, Muskimgun, Muskoka, Muskwa, Nakota, Nanaimo, Nantucket, Napa, Narragansett, Natchez, Naugatuck, Navajo, Nebraska, Niagara, Norwalk, Ocala, Ohio, Okanagan, Okeechobee, Oklahoma, Omaha, Omak, Oneida, Onondaga, Ontario, Oregon, Orono, Osage, Oswego, Ottawa, Palouse, Pamlico, Panola, Pataha, Pawnee, Pennacook, Pennamaquan, Pensacola, Penticton, Peoga, Peoria, Peotone, Pequot, Pocahontas, Poconos, Pontiac,

Potomac, Potosi, Poughkeepsie, Quebec, Rappahannock, Roanoke, Sarasota, Saratoga, Saskatchewan, Saskatoon, Savannah, Sawhatchee, Scituate, Seattle, Sebago, Seneca, Sequoia, Seminole, Sewanee, Shannock, Shawnee, Shenandoah, Shetucket, Shiboygan, Shoshone, Sicamous, Sioux, Siska, Sonoma, Sowanee, Spokane, Squamish, Squaw, Stawamus, Sunapee, Susquehanna, Swannanoa, Tacoma, Taconic, Tahoe, Takoma, Tallahassee, Tampa, Tecumseh, Tennessee, Texarcana, Texas, Tichigan, Ticonderoga, Tippecanoe, Tomahawk, Topawingo, Topeka, Toronto, Tucson, Tulsa, Tunica, Tuscaloosa, Tuscarora, Tuskegee, Tuya, Utah, Ute, Wabamun, Wabasca, Wabash, Waco, Wadena Walla Walla, Wallowa, Wanakit, Wanchese, Wannock, Wapota, Wasco, Watauga, Watonga, Waupaca, Wausau, Wenatchee, Wenonah, Wichita, Willamette, Winnebago, Winnimac, Winnipeg, Winona, Wisconsin, Wyoming, Yakutat, Yazoo, Yosemite, Yuba, Yukon, Yuma . . .

What language do these sonorous names speak? What message do they convey to us? Indigenous names are indicators of the prior habitations of the First Nations who lived and prospered in the rich lands of the Americas, from the Atlantic to the Pacific, from the Caribbean to Alaska. Anthropologists estimate that some ten million human beings resided in North America when their lands were "discovered" by the Europeans. This vast continent was theirs, full of villages, wigwams, tipis, laughter and life. Where are these people now? Today American Indian numbers are estimated at 2.9 million.[66] Where have all the others gone? Gone and forgotten, blown with the wind and the clouds.

---

66 Out of the total U.S. population, 2.9 million people, or 0.9 percent, reported American Indian or Alaska Native alone. In addition, 2.3 million people or another 0.7 percent, reported American Indian or Alaska Native in combination with one or more other races. Together, these two groups totaled 5.2 million people. Thus, 1.7 percent of all people in the United States identified as American Indian or Alaska Native, either alone or in combination with one or more other races.

Let us pause and reflect on what indigenous place names in Central and South America tell us:

What does Chapultepec, Chichen Itza, Cuba, Machu Picchu, Tikal and Ushuaia tell us? That south of the Rio Grande the continent was populated by millions of human beings, perhaps as many as 70 million. Their land was not *terra nullius*. We can still recognize the Aztec, the Maya, the Inca, the Quechua in the populations of Central and South America. The indigenous of South America are still very much there, numbering possibly as many as 40 million, and gradually they are demanding their rights back. The election of Evo Morales, an Aymara indigenous person, to the Presidency of Bolivia in 2006 marked the election of the first indigenous president of a Latin American country.

From the writings of the Dominican friars Bartolomé de las Casas and Antonio de Montesinos we have learned that the Arawacs, the Siboneyes and Tainos were massacred and enslaved. How many indigenous lives were deliberately extinguished by the European colonizers? How many died or disease and deprivation? Ten million? Twenty?

Let us revisit what indigenous place names in North and South America mean:

Alaska means "great land" in Aleutian
Allegheny means "beautiful stream" in Lenape language
Apalachee means "other side of the river" in Muskogean
Chesapeake means "great shellfish bay" in Algonquin
Chicago means "place of the wild onion" in Algonquin
Cuba means "fertile land" in Arawakan Taino language
Illinois means "ordinary speaker" in Algonquin
Iowa means "sleepy ones" in Algonquin
Kansas means "Southwind" in Sioux language
Kentucky means "meadow" in Shawnee
Manhattan means "island" in Lenape language
Massachusetts means "large hill place" in Algonquin
Mississippi means "big river" in Algonquin
Missouri means "people of the big canoes" in Algonquin

Nebraska means "flat river" in Sioux language
Niagara means "Thundering water" in Iroquois
Ohio means "good river" in Iroquois
Ontario means "beautiful lake" in Iroquois
Ottawa means "trading centre" in Algonquin
Pensacola means "hair-people" in Muskogean
Potomac means "something brought" in Algonquin
Quebec means "straits" or "narrows" in Micmac
Toronto means "meeting place" in Huron
Ushuaia means "deep bay" in Yaghan
Wallowa means "winding water" in Sahaptin language
Winnipeg means "dirty water" in Algonquin
Wyoming means "at the big plains" in Algonquin

Perhaps the new recognition of the horror of slavery and the oppression of Afro-Americans may open our eyes to the genocide against Native Americans, whom we call "Indians" rather than by the distinct names by which these peoples call themselves, will motivate us to come to grips with the on-going looting of the natural resources of the North and South American Indigenous, acknowledge the gross injustices committed against them and prompt us to consider how to ensure adequate reparation and sustainable rehabilitation.

In 1964 Martin Luther King, Jr. attempted to draw attention to the tragedy of Native Americans. In his book "*Why We Can't Wait*," he wrote:

Our nation was born in genocide when it embraced the doctrine that the original American, the Indian, was an inferior race. Even before there were large numbers of Negroes on our shores, the scar of racial hatred had already disfigured colonial society. From the sixteenth century forward, blood flowed in battles over racial supremacy. We are perhaps the only nation which tried as a matter of national policy to wipe out its indigenous population. Moreover, we elevated that tragic experience into a noble crusade. Indeed, even today we have not permitted ourselves to reject or to feel remorse for this shameful episode. Our literature, our films, our drama, our folklore all exalt it.[67]

For an average American, these words are tough to read. Unfortunately, these words correspond with lived reality. That is perhaps why this aspect of Martin Luther King's legacy is systematically ignored by the media, why it is not taught in high schools and universities. I sincerely hope that one day history will give credit to Dr. King for taking up the cause of the indigenous.

Nearly sixty years after Dr. King wrote those words, racism against indigenous Americans persists, and many do not forget the signs that used to hang in South Dakota stores—in Arizona near the Navajo "Reservation" and in so many other places in the American West: "No dogs or Indians allowed."[68] This kind of humiliation is difficult to forget.

Let us hope that politicians listen, recognize the immensity of the crime against the indigenous peoples of North and South America and make an effort to rehabilitate the survivors, giving them at the very least the rights enunciated in the UN Declaration on the Rights of Indigenous Peoples.[69]

67 Martin Luther King, *Why We Can't Wait* (1964), New York: New American Library (Harper & Row). pp. 118–19.

68 Evelyn Red Lodge, "Racism against Native Americans persists" (opinion), *High Country News,* September 21, 2017, https://www.hcn.org/issues/49.17/opinion-racism-against-native-americans-persists; Kirby Neumann-Rea, "'The story has another chapter': first Indigenous Peoples' Day observed," *Columbia Gorge News,* October 12, 2016 (updated July 27, 2020), https://www.columbiagorgenews.com/archive/the-story-has-another-chapter-first-indigenous-peoples-day-observed/article_ef115dbe-b3b4-596e-9e35-7b9b95f5f112.html; J. Weston Phippen, "In Gallup, surrounded by the Navajo Nation, a pandemic crosses paths with homelessness, hate and healersm," *NM Political Report,* June 22, 2020, https://nmpoliticalreport.com/2020/06/22/in-gallup-surrounded-by-the-navajo-nation-a-pandemic-crosses-paths-with-homelessness-hate-and-healers/; "Native Americans Protest Flier," *Los Angeles Times,* November 2, 2004, https://www.latimes.com/archives/la-xpm-2004-nov-02-na-trailmix2-story.html

69 https://www.un.org/development/desa/indigenouspeoples/declaration-on-

RECENT SCHOLARLY RESEARCH ON INDIGENOUS ISSUES

In recent years important scholarly studies have been published that should make us pause and reassess how we look at history and how it impacts today's world. Among such books are David Stannard's groundbreaking *American Holocaust* (Oxford, 1992) and Tamara Starblanket's more recent *Suffer the Little Children: Genocide, Indigenous Nations and the Canadian State* (Clarity Press, 2018)[70] revealing the continuing process of the physical and cultural extinction of the Original Nations of North America.

The potential of these books would be achieved if historians and the media were committed to comprehensive truth in the correct context and if they would abandon double standards, selective indignation and that most effective weapon: silence. *Damnatio memoriae* occurred not only in Greek and Roman times,[71] it has been practiced by all civilizations. Ours continues the tradition through direct and indirect censorship. Perhaps the recent scandals concerning the unmarked graves in Canadian residential schools[72] for indigenous children will encourage

---

the-rights-of-indigenous-peoples.html

70   What follows is excerpted from my review of Starblanket's ground-breaking work, which appeared in the *Netherlands Journal of International Law* in September 2021, which referenced the following:

S. Benoist, *Mémoire et histoire: les procédures de condamnation dans l'antiquité romaine* (Centre régional universitaire lorrain d'histoire, 2007*);* Denevan W. Metz (ed.) *The Native Population of the Americas in 1492* (Madison, Wisconsin: University of Wisconsin Press, 1992); H. Dobyns, "Estimating aboriginal American population: An appraisal of techniques with a new hemispheric estimate," *Current Anthropology* 7(4):395–416 (1966); R. Lemkin, *Axis Rule in Occupied Europe* (Washington, D.C.: Carnegie Endowment for International Peace, 1944); R. Lemkin, *Genocide: A Modern Crime* (New York: Free World, 1945); S.T. Newcomb, "The UN Declaration on the Rights of Indigenous Peoples and the paradigm of domination," *Griffith Law Review* 20:578–607 (2011); S.H. Venne, *Our Elders Understand Our Rights: Evolving International Law Regarding Indigenous Peoples' Rights* (Penticton, B.C.: Theytus Books, 1998).

71   Benoist (2007).

72   "The Residential School System," Parks Canada, Government of Canada, https://www.canada.ca/en/parks-canada/news/2020/09/the-residential-school-system.html (accessed May 25, 2022). Such schools also existed in the U.S. In May

historians and legal scholars to conduct research into the "clash of civilizations" associated with the colonization of North and South America.[73]

An incisive foreword to Tamara Starblanket's book by history professor Ward Churchill and a strong epilogue by international law expert Sharon Venne[74] make Starblanket's brilliant dissertation a political manifesto, a call for action to restore the human rights of the Original Nations of Canada, especially their right of self-determination, which has been and continues to be violated by the colonizers, the Canadian settler society. In this timely and morally necessary book, Starblanket gives particular attention to the forced transfer of indigenous children to institutions whose raison d'être was to indoctrinate and "educate" them away from their culture and heritage so as to erase indigenous memory and reprogram the younger generation as "Canadians." These institutions were notorious for death and disease, torture, forced starvation, forced labour and sexual predation.

2022 the U.S. Department of the Interior published an official report, which probes into occurrences in the "Indian Schools" in the U.S., where indigenous children had been forcibly taken away from their families and tribes in order to forcibly assimilate them. Among other things the investigation uncovered that over 500 students had died while attending one of 408 boarding schools for native Americans, Alaska natives and native Hawaiian children, established or run by the U.S. government in the 19th and 20th centuries. The intent of such schools was nothing less than cultural genocide. See Bryan Newland, *Federal Indian Boarding School Initiative Investigative Report,* U.S. Department of the Interior, May 2022, https://www.bia.gov/sites/default/files/dup/inline-files/bsi_investigative_report_may_2022_508.pdf

73 "Canada: More unmarked graves likely at former residential school site," *BBC News,* July 15, 2021, https://www.bbc.com/news/world-us-canada-57855952 (accessed August 3, 2021); D. Lao, "People complicit in Canada's residential school deaths should be charged, group says," *Global News,* June 24, 2021, https://globalnews.ca/news/7978394/canada-residential-school-criminal-charges/ (accessed August 3, 2021); Leyland Cecco, "Canada discovers 751 unmarked graves at former residential school," *The Guardian,* June 24, 2021, https://www.theguardian.com/world/2021/jun/24/canada-school-graves-discovery-saskatchewan (accessed August 3, 2021).

74 Venne (1998).

Starblanket begins by addressing the catastrophe that befell the Original Nations, victims of a relentless colonial assault on their existence as "peoples," characterized by massacres, expropriations, expulsions, and the imposition of conditions of life aimed at their destruction. Starblanket puts emphasis not only on the physical destruction of peoples, but on the concept of cultural genocide, which was so important to Raphael Lemkin, who coined the term "genocide" in 1944,[75] and who clearly intended to have it apply to the attempt to destroy a people's culture, identity, and traditions. The States parties that adopted the Genocide Convention on December 9, 1948, however, intended to continue their colonial practices of cultural genocide and thus dropped the concept of denying a people the right to their own culture and way of life, although this very right is protected by the UNESCO Constitution[76] and by the subsequent UNESCO Convention on the Protection and Promotion of the Diversity of Cultural Expressions.[77]

She also addresses the wall of evasion and denial surrounding the ongoing crime against Indigenous Peoples, quoting Harold Cardinal, a survivor of the residential schools: "The policies adopted by Canada over the years with regard to Indians are not different from the rationale employed by Nazi Germany in its implementation of what is called the 'Final Solution.' Residential schools were only one element." Yet, the rubrics of denial are many.

Chapter 1 focuses on the definition of genocide and its application to Indigenous Peoples. Chapter 2 describes the deliberate policies of separating indigenous children from their parents and the attempt at making true "Canadians" out of them. There are many "smoking guns" that point at the "intention" to destroy the

---

75 Lemkin (1944) and (1945).

76 See http://portal.unesco.org/en/ev.php-URL_ID=15244%26URL_DO=DO_TOPIC%26URL_SECTION=201.html and http://www.unesco.org/education/pdf/UNESCO_E.PDF.

77 See https://en.unesco.org/creativity/convention (accessed August 3, 2021).

indigenous culture. As Duncan Campbell Scott, Superintendent of the Department of Indian Affairs, wrote: "I want to get rid of the Indian problem [...] Our objective is to continue until there is not a single Indian in Canada that has not been absorbed into the body politic and there is no Indian question." One may add that Campbell added insult to injury by referring to an "Indian" problem, when he meant the right of identity of the Original Nations of Canada—the Algonquin, the Cree, the Lingit, the Mi'kmaq, the Mohawk, the Oneida, and the Squamish—none of them inhabitants of the Indian Sub-continent!

Chapter 3 reviews the history of Canada as a colonizing State and analyses the phenomenon of "cognitive condition-ing" (pp. 160 et seq.). Starblanket cites an insightful study by Steven Newcomb, Director of the Indigenous Law Institute, on the UN Declaration on the Rights of Indigenous Peoples[78] and the paradigm of domination.[79] It is important to understand the unseen assumptions in colonial law, the media, and academia concerning the Original Nations of North America and the use of metaphors: "Cognitive theory enables us to realize that [Western] law is the result of non-indigenous cognitive pro-cesses, social practices and conventions, and cultural patterns, and of the way that members of the dominating society imagi-natively project taken-for-granted categories and concepts onto indigenous peoples" of which the "overall effect has been the traumatic intergenerational domination of [Indigenous Peoples'] existence" (p. 161).

Chapter 4 is aptly titled "Smoke and Mirrors. Canada's Pretence of Compliance with the Genocide Convention." She cites Eli Wiesel's famous book *Night*: "They are committing

---

78 The text of the declaration can be found at https://www.un.org/development/desa/indigenouspeoples/declaration-on-the-rights-of-indigenous-peoples.html (accessed August 3, 2021).

79 Steven T. Newcomb, *Pagans in the Promised Land: Decoding the Doctrine of Christian Discovery* (Chicago Review Press/Fulcrum, 2008), a bestseller on Amazon. Newcomb is co-producer of *The Doctrine of Discovery: Unmasking the Domination Code,* directed by Sheldon Wolfchild (Dakota).

the greatest indignity human beings can inflict on one another: telling people who have suffered excruciating pain and loss that their pain and loss were illusions" (p. 206). Indeed, society and the media have been in denial of the crimes committed and still being committed against Indigenous Peoples. It is a kind of negationism, which, unlike the vulgar negationism of the Holocaust, is more or less socially acceptable in the U.S. and Canada. Starblanket refers to Article II of the Genocide Convention and cites the five acts "committed with the intent to destroy, in whole or in part, a national, ethnical, racial or religious group, as such: a) killing members of the group; b) causing serious bodily or mental harm to members of the group; c) deliberately inflicting on the group conditions of life calculated to bring about its physical destruction in whole or in part; d) imposing measures intended to prevent births within the group; e) forcibly transferring children of the group to another group."[80] She shows how these violations have been perpetrated against Indigenous Peoples and describes the forcible transfer of indigenous children, which Prime Minister Harper blandly referred to as "profoundly negative" and therefore "wrong" (p. 220). Yet, is "wrong" not a far cry from criminal? Is it a subterfuge to avoid the possibility of legal recourse and remedy?

There is an urgent need to rehabilitate the indigenous communities and to give them the necessary financing and space to allow them to reconstruct their lives and their future. Notwithstanding the lip service being paid to the rights of the indigenous, to ILO Convention 169, to the UN Declaration on the Rights of Indigenous Peoples, there is little or no conviction behind governmental pronouncements and the ultimate goal remains the "assimilation" of the remaining Indigenous Peoples after their respective cultures have been extinguished. There is something unnatural about the Canadian government's "Truth

---

80 See UN General Assembly resolution 260 A (III), "Convention on the Prevention and Punishment of the Crime of Genocide," https://www.ohchr.org/en/professionalinterest/pages/crimeofgenocide.aspx (accessed August 3, 2021).

and Reconciliation Commission," which in a real sense constitutes "a safety valve, enabling recognition without facing legal culpability," because of the built-in legal loopholes and other intellectual maneuvers.

Surely everyone needs truth—most urgently the non-indigenous, 99% of whom have no conception of the monstruous crimes committed and still being committed against Indigenous Peoples—not only in Canada, but in the United States, Brazil, Chile, Colombia, Guatemala, Honduras, etc. In her conclusion, Starblanket reminds us that "the non-indigenous scholar is unable to conceive of his/her complicity in the brutal or destructive nature of colonialism, and furthermore cannot conceive that the problem exists in the society that allows horrific acts of violence against the innocent to continue." One would think that "there is no sugar-coating genocide," but the fact remains that the suppression of information leads to the suppression of thought, of empathy, of the inner voice that tells us that something must be done. Truth requires not only an "apology" followed by "business as usual," but a commitment to try to make some sort of reparation. This reviewer strongly agrees with Starblanket's assessment that "so-called state solutions cloaked in euphemisms and rhetoric such as 'reconciliation' only further the colonial agenda. [...] For indigenous Peoples who have undergone genocidal acts, reconciliation is an oxymoron. The illusion that Indigenous Peoples are now achieving justice must be dispelled." The problem remains that there is no genuine remorse, but only public relations exercises aimed at distracting attention and sowing confusion.

As with the Holocaust, all the billions of German marks and Euros paid by Germany to the victims of Nazism cannot undo the atrocities, but at least it is recognition, not a cover-up or a whitewash. It evidences that moral responsibility has been awakened. In the case of the descendants of the ten million Indigenous Peoples of North America,[81] there remains a legal

---

81 Dobyns (1966); Denevan (ed.) (1992).

and moral obligation to make reparation, which would amount to many billions (not to say trillions) of dollars in compensation for the genocide that accompanied the deadliest "clash of civilizations."

The late UN Special Rapporteur of the Sub-commission on Promotion and Protection of Human Rights, Professor Miguel Alfonso Martinez, expressed a caveat that "it is not possible to undo all that has been done [...] but this does not negate the ethical imperative to undo (even at the expense, if need be, of the straightjacket imposed by the unbending observance of the 'rule of [non-indigenous] law') the wrongs [crimes] done both spiritually and materially, to the Indigenous Peoples" (p. 269). I would like to be bolder and say that there must be a "road map" designed by Indigenous Peoples and supported by the Office of the UN High Commissioner for Human Rights to make rehabilitation and reparation happen.

The way ahead must be built on the imperative of implementing the right of self-determination for all peoples on this planet. As Professor Miguel Alfonso Martinez wrote in his final report entitled "Study on treaties, agreements and other constructive arrangements between States and indigenous populations,"[82] Indigenous Peoples are entitled to the inalienable right of self-determination, which is enshrined in Article 1 of the UN Charter, Article 1 of the Covenant on Civil and Political Rights, and Article 2 of the Covenant on Economic, Social and Cultural Rights. This right *of* (and not just "to") self-determination belongs to that category of peremptory international law principles known as *jus cogens*. The reviewer's 2013 report to the Human Rights Council quotes extensively from Alfonso's report,[83] as well as the 2014 report to the General

---

82 Miguel Alfonso Martínez, Special Rapporteur, *Human Rights of Indigenous Peoples: Study on treaties, agreements and other constructive arrangements between States and indigenous populations*, June 22, 1999, UN Doc. E/CN.4/Sub.2/1999/20, https://undocs.org/en/E/CN.4/Sub.2/1999/20 (accessed August 3, 2021).

83 See Annex XIII in "Report of the Independent Expert on the promotion of a democratic and equitable international order, Alfred-Maurice de Zayas,"

Assembly, which is devoted entirely to the theory and practice of self-determination,[84] and in the 2018 report to the Human Rights Council, which formulates 25 Principles of International Order, including the implementation of the right of self-determination as a conflict-prevention measure.[85]

Starblanket challenges the reader to reassess mainstream "certainties" and "values," to test whether Western "enlightened" societies and mainstream human rights activists are practicing what they preach. The book holds a mirror to every reader and invites him/her to come to grips with fundamental issues of natural justice, exploitation, discrimination, humiliation, impunity for genocide and crimes against humanity.

What can we learn from this book? Perhaps the bottom line is that colonization by the Europeans has never ended. There was no decolonization process like in Africa or Asia. To this day the Indigenous Peoples of North America continue to live in a form of colonial subjugation, and unlike the peoples of Africa and Asia, the Original Nations of the United States and Canada were never restored to independence and prosperity, partly because the Original Nations were victims of physical genocide and the European settlers became so numerous that the Indigenous Peoples became minorities in their own lands, their natural resources being looted by the European migrants. Only the indigenous names of the rivers, mountains, lakes, cities and villages remain as testimony of their existence.

In a world plagued by fake news, fake history and fake law, it is remarkable that this intellectually honest work was originally

---

A/HRC/24/38, January 7, 2013, https://ap.ohchr.org/documents/dpage_e.aspx?si=A/HRC/24/38 (accessed August 3, 2021).

84 See "Promotion of a democratic and equitable international order," Note by the Secretary-General to the UN General Assembly [A/69/272], August 7, 2014, https://www.un.org/ga/search/viewm_doc.asp?symbol=A/69/272 (accessed August 3, 2021).

85 See "Report of the Independent Expert on the promotion of a democratic and equitable international order - Note by the Secretariat," January 25, 2018, https://ap.ohchr.org/documents/dpage_e.aspx?si=A/HRC/37/63 (accessed August 3, 2021).

a dissertation accepted by the University of Saskatchewan in a conformist academic environment. This gives reason for mitigated optimism. Her book is a *tour de force*, important not only for Indigenous Peoples, but especially for the non-indigenous who may be moved to action based on the common humanity of all members of the human family, who believe that natural justice requires affirmative action to begin restoring Indigenous Peoples to a position that will guarantee the survival of their ancient culture and traditions. Perhaps Canada should consider nominating indigenous traditions as "intangible cultural heritage of mankind"[86] and take the necessary measures to preserve them.

---

86 See "What is Intangible Cultural Heritage?," UNESCO/Intangible Cultural Heritage, https://ich.unesco.org/en/what-is-intangible-heritage-00003 (accessed August 3, 2021).

18.

The U.S. Naval Base at Guantánamo: Indefinite Detention, Torture, Belligerent Occupation[87]

HISTORICAL BACKGROUND

Guantánamo Naval base is the oldest American naval base outside the continental United States. It occupies 45 square miles, or 117.6 square kilometres, an area roughly the size of Manhattan Island. It is situated in the southeast corner of Cuba's easternmost Oriente Province, west of Haiti and north of Jamaica. It has been continuously occupied by the United States since the Spanish-American war in 1898 and played a role in U.S. monitoring of the Caribbean seas during the first and second world wars. Guantánamo played a role in the logistics for the 1983 United States invasion of Grenada, the 1984 invasion of Haiti, and the 1989 invasion of Panama. Other than for such adventures, Guantánamo has scarce strategic significance. The base was significantly expanded in 1951, 1964, 1991 and 2002 and is totally self-sufficient with its own power and water sources.

Pursuant to a commitment undertaken by the Cuban Constitutional Assembly in 1901, Cuba agreed to include in its Constitution the text of the so-called "Platt Amendment" (*Enmienda Platt*), in exchange for which the United States would withdraw its occupation troops from Cuba. By virtue of the *Enmienda* the United States had the right to intervene

---

87 A much shorter version of this article was published in the *Max Planck Encyclopedia of Public International Law* IV (Oxford, Englnd: Oxford University Press, 2012), 632–636.

militarily in the domestic affairs of Cuba and Cuba was obliged
to grant naval bases to the United States. Before the *Enmienda*
was abrogated in 1934, the United States intervened militarily in
Cuba on five occasions, notably in 1912 and 1917, employing
the troops already stationed at the naval base.

On May 20, 1902 Cuba was declared independent and
Tomas Estrada Palma, a United States citizen, became President.
In 1903 Estrada Palma signed a first lease agreement over naval
bases in Guantánamo and Bahia Honda; a second lease agreement
followed in 1934. Since the Cuban revolution of 1959, Cuba has
maintained that the United States occupation of Guantánamo
is illegal and a vestige of colonialism. To emphasize the point,
since 1960 Cuba has not cashed the annual checks in the amount
of $4,085 tendered by the United States as rent for the use of the
territory. In October 1960, the United States imposed a partial
embargo on Cuba, which became a total embargo in February
1962. Official diplomatic relations were severed by the United
States in January 1961.

Cuba has repeatedly protested against the continued United
States presence in Guantánamo before the General Assembly
and the UN Commission on Human Rights. On August 18, 2007
Cuban President Fidel Castro set out the Cuban legal claims
against the United States and placed them in historical context,
indicating, however, that force would never be used to recover
Guantánamo. Cuban protests notwithstanding, the United States
has asserted its intention to stay indefinitely in Guantánamo,
which for purposes of a self-serving interpretation of United
States constitutional law permits it to serve as a "legal black
hole," formally outside the sovereign territory of the United
States but entirely under its jurisdiction and control. Although
leased as a naval and coaling station, the base was used in the
1990s for housing more than 50,000 Haitian and Cuban refugees
and economic migrants, and since January 2002 it has been converted into a detention and interrogation centre for more than
700 prisoners of war and suspected terrorists.

LEASE AGREEMENTS

Article VII of the Platt Amendment stipulates, "That to enable the United States to maintain the independence of Cuba, and to protect the people thereof, as well as for its own defense, the government of Cuba shall sell or lease to the United States lands necessary for coaling or naval stations at certain specified points to be agreed upon with the President of the United States." Article VIII stipulates: "That by way of further assurance the government of Cuba will embody the foregoing provisions in a permanent treaty with the United States." This agreement was imposed on the incipient Cuban administration as a condition to the departure of the United States military that had been occupying Cuba since the 1898 Spanish-American War. It was pursuant to the Platt Amendment that the 1903 lease agreement was signed, obligating Cuba to lease "for the time required for the purposes of coaling and naval stations," several "areas of land and water situated in the Island of Cuba" (article 1), including Guantánamo. Under article II, Cuba granted "the right to use and occupy the waters adjacent to said areas of land and water . . . and generally to do any and all things necessary to fit the premises for use as coaling or naval stations only, *and for no other purpose*" (emphasis added).

With regard to the issue of sovereignty, Article III stipulates: "While on the one hand the United States recognizes the *continuance of the ultimate sovereignty of the Republic of Cuba* over the above described areas of land and water, on the other hand the Republic of Cuba consents that during the period of the occupation by the United States of said areas under the terms of this agreement, the United States shall exercise *complete jurisdiction and control* over and within said areas with the right to acquire for the public purposes of the United States any land or other property therein by purchase or by exercise of eminent domain with full compensation to the owners thereof."

This Agreement was signed by Cuban president, Tomás Estrada Palma, on February 16, 1903 and by the president of the United States, Theodore Roosevelt, one week later. It was then supplemented by a further agreement signed by the plenipotentiaries of Cuba and the United States on July 2, 1903. Pursuant to article I of this supplementary Convention, the United States agreed to pay to the Republic of Cuba the annual sum of two thousand dollars. Article 2 further stipulates that "no person, partnership, or corporation shall be permitted to establish or maintain a commercial, industrial or other enterprise within said areas."

The 1903 agreements were confirmed and slightly revised by a new treaty, signed in Washington on May 29, 1934, in which the United States agreed to increase the amount of the lease from $2,000 to $4,085 per annum. With regard to the duration of the lease, Article III of the 1934 agreement provides that "Until the two Contracting Parties agree to the modification or abrogation of the stipulations of the Agreement in regard to the lease to the United States of America of lands in Cuba for coaling and naval stations . . . the stipulations of that Agreement with regard to the naval station of Guantánamo shall continue in effect."

CUBAN AND UNITED STATES
VIEWS ON THE LEASE

In 1959 the Cuban Government informed the United States that the lease should be terminated, expressing the view that the continued United States presence in Guantánamo constituted an illegal occupation. For this reason, the Cuban Government has not cashed the lease cheques since 1960. Following the Cuban missile crisis in 1962, President Fidel Castro presented a plan of reconciliation with the United States. Point Five of the "Cinco Puntos" advanced on October 28, 1962 as a basis for negotiations stipulates the "withdrawal from the Guantánamo Naval Base . . . and return of the Cuban territory occupied by the United States."

In January 2002, shortly after the United States started trans-ferring Taliban detainees to Guantánamo, the Government of Cuba made a declaration recalling that: "The Platt Amendment, which granted the United States the right to intervene in Cuba, was imposed on the text of our 1901 Constitution as a prerequi-site for the withdrawal of the American troops from the Cuban territory. In line with that clause, the aforementioned Agreement on Coaling and Naval Stations was signed in February 1903. . . . In due course . . . the illegally occupied territory of Guantánamo should be returned to Cuba." In a statement to the General Assembly dated June 14, 2002, Cuba demanded that the United States return Guantánamo, noting that the territory had been "usurped illegally against the wishes of its people." On January 19, 2005 Cuba presented a note verbale to the United States protesting against the misuse of the Naval Base for other than "naval and coaling" purposes and accusing the United States of committing grave human rights violations on Cuban soil. Of the 780 detainees, including minors, who were kept under a regime of indefinite detention[88] in Guantánamo since the begin-ning of the "war on terror." some 37 detainees still remain in Guantánamo.[89] Many were subjected to torture.[90]

The United States has repeatedly stated that it intends to stay indefinitely in Guantánamo and is currently expanding the base. It advances a positivist legal approach to the continued validity of the lease, insisting that it is open-ended in duration and that it can be terminated only by mutual agreement. According to this approach, for as long as the United States withholds its con-sent to termination, it effectively exercises not only complete

88 Alfred de Zayas, "Human rights and indefinite detention," *International Review of the Red Cross* 87:857, March 2005, https://www.icrc.org/en/doc/assets/files/other/irrc_857_zayas.pdf.

89 "The Guantánamo Docket," *The New York Times,* updated May 5, 2022, https://www.nytimes.com/interactive/2021/us/guantanamo-bay-detainees.html.

90 Bridge Initiative Team, "FACTSHEET: Torture at Guantánamo Bay Detention Camp," July 19, 2020, https://bridge.georgetown.edu/research/factsheet-torture-at-guantanamo-bay-detention-camp/.

jurisdiction over the area, but effectively all the trappings of sovereignty. If it were to do so, this would render Guantánamo a quasi-dependent territory of the United States.

VALIDITY OF THE LEASE AGREEMENT
UNDER INTERNATIONAL LAW

In interpreting the validity of the lease agreement, there are three possible scenarios: lease in perpetuity, void *ex tunc*, and voidable *ex nunc*.

A. Lease in perpetuity

Article 26 of the *Vienna Convention on the Law of Treaties* (VCLT) stipulates that every treaty in force is binding upon the parties and must be performed by them in good faith: *Pacta sunt servanda*. On its terms, the Guantánamo treaty is still valid, and Cuba has no choice but to respect its continued validity, since Cuba failed to secure its rights by clearly stipulating a date of termination. Thus, as long as the United States insists on its continuation, Cuba cannot rescind it. The official position of the United States is that it has a perpetual lease, since article 1 of the 1934 lease agreement provides that the lease can be revised or terminated only by mutual agreement. This position is reflected in the judgments of United States federal courts that interpret the lease agreement as a valid perpetual lease, in which Cuba has ultimate sovereignty but the United States has full jurisdiction. This positivist approach to international law was generally practiced in the early twentieth century, but it is no longer compatible with modern international law, particularly in the light of the law of de-colonization and the recent experience of the termination of other comparable "perpetual" leases.

B. Void ex tunc

According to this scenario, the lease agreement may be considered to have been void from the beginning, because it was imposed by force. Pursuant to article 52 VCLT: "A treaty is void if its conclusion has been procured by the threat or use of force in violation of the principles of international law embodied in the Charter of the United Nations." Although the VCLT only entered into force in 1980 and the United States is not a party to it, most of its provisions, including article 52, are recognized as declarative of pre-existing international law. However, the question arises whether the prohibition of force or the prohibition of annexation had already coagulated as a norm of international law in 1903 or in 1934, when the lease agreements were signed. The evidence from State practice shows that the prohibition on the use of force and the prohibition of coercion had not yet emerged in 1903, so that even the annexation of Cuba in 1903 would have been conceivable in the light of the unsettled state of turn-of-the century international law, the hey-day of imperialism and colonialism, of the Monroe Doctrine and "manifest destiny." According to the inter-temporal law principle enunciated by the Permanent Court of International Justice in the *Island of Palmas Arbitration* (2 R.I.A.A. 829, 4 I.L.R. 3, 1928), it is the law in existence at the relevant time (1903, 1934 for the Guantánamo leases) that governs the question of the validity of the treaty or the question of sovereignty at that point in time. In the light of these considerations, it is difficult to conclude that the lease agreements were void *ab initio*.

C. Voidable ex nunc

A third scenario is that, while the lease may have been valid *ab initio*, it is now voidable. In this connection the doctrine of "unequal treaties" becomes particularly relevant. While not challenging the validity of the treaty from the start or the legality of actions taken pursuant to the treaty, it allows for its termination today. Article 64 VCLT stipulates that if a new peremptory norm of general international law emerges, any existing treaty that is in conflict with that norm becomes void. Self-determination is such a peremptory norm, as illustrated in the de-colonization process. Moreover, article 1 of the *International Covenant on*

Civil and Political Rights, and article 1 of the International Covenant on Economic, Social and Cultural Rights both stipulate the right to self-determination and the right of a people to dispose of its natural wealth and resources. General Assembly Resolution 1514 (XV) *Declaration on the granting of independence to colonial countries and peoples* (GA Res. 1514(XV) UN GAOR 15th Sess., December 14, 1960) affirms the right to self-determination and stipulates in paragraph 6 that "any attempt aimed at the partial or total disruption of the national unity and the territorial integrity of a country is incompatible with the purposes and principles of the Charter of the United Nations." On the occasion of the adoption of this Resolution, the Cuban Foreign Minister Raul Roa stated that this declaration necessarily applied to Guantánamo Naval Base. Similarly, the United Nations *Declaration on Principles of International Law concerning Friendly Relations and Co-operation among States in accordance with the Charter of the United Nations* (GA Res. 2625 (XXV), UN GAOR, 25th Sess., UN Doc. A/8082 (1970), affirms the principle of equal rights of peoples and the principle of the sovereign equality of States.

As to the issue of duress in the lease agreements of 1903 and 1934, it is worth recalling that in 1969 the Vienna Conference on the Law of Treaties adopted a "Declaration on the Prohibition of Military, Political or Economic Coercion in the Conclusion of Treaties" by virtue of which the Conference proclaimed that it: "Solemnly condemns the threat or use of pressure in any form, whether military, political, or economic, by any state in order to coerce another State to perform any act relating to the conclusion of a treaty in violation of the principles of the sovereign equality of States and freedom of consent.."

In the light of the above, five possible grounds for invalidating the lease agreement become apparent: (i) the doctrine of unequal treaties; (ii) the emergence of a peremptory norm of international law which is incompatible with the lease agreement; (iii) implied right of denunciation; (iv) the doctrine of fundamental change of circumstances; and (v) termination by virtue of material breach of the terms of the lease.

(i) Doctrine of Unequal Treaties

The process of de-colonization in the United Nations gave impetus to the doctrine of the invalidity of unequal treaties. This doctrine has been confirmed by the renegotiation of the Panama Canal in 1977 and its return to Panamanian sovereignty in January 2000. Based on the same doctrine, the United Kingdom returned Hong Kong to China in 1997 and Portugal returned Macau to China in 1999. Although the relevant treaties and lease agreements were originally declared to be "in perpetuity" by the United States, the United Kingdom and Portugal, respectively, they were terminated by subsequent peaceful negotiation. In arguing for the return of Hong Kong and Macau, China specifically invoked the doctrine of "unequal treaties."

In his 1947 course at the Hague Academy, Serge Krylov, judge at the International Court of Justice, expressed the view that unequal treaties and those establishing capitulary regimes "by which an imperialist power imposes its will upon a weaker state" are invalid. Professor F. I. Kozhevnikov expresses the same view in his textbook on international law, in which he states: "The principle that international treaties must be observed does not extend to treaties which are imposed by force, and which are unequal in character.... Equal treaties are treaties concluded on the basis of the equality of the parties.... Unequal treaties are not legally binding.... Treaties must be based upon the sovereign equality of the contracting parties."

Applying this principle to Guantánamo, it is undisputed that in 1902 Cuba was a kind of "protectorate" of the United States, and not a sovereign State when it emerged from four years of United States military occupation. It was handicapped by the imposition of the Platt Amendment, which granted to the United States the right to interfere in its internal affairs. Thus, the unequal treaties are voidable in terms of modern international law.

(ii) Emergence of New Peremptory Norms

After the Second World War, in the light of the process of de-colonization, the principle of self-determination has emerged as *jus cogens*. Hence, article 64 VCLT provides that "if a new peremptory norm of general international law emerges, any existing treaty which is in conflict with that norm becomes void and terminates." Thus, treaties in violation of the principle of self-determination, many of which were imposed upon weak nations by strong nations in the age of imperialism, may be deemed invalid if *jus cogens* can be shown to have been violated. The return of the Panama Canal to Panamanian sovereignty is illustrative of this rule.

In paragraph 11 of Resolution 2189 (XXI), "Implementation of the Declaration on the Granting of Independence to Colonial Countries and Peoples" of December 13, 1966, the UN General Assembly requested "the colonial Powers to dismantle their military bases and installations in colonial Territories and to refrain from establishing new ones and from using those that still exist to interfere with the liberation of the peoples in colonial Territories in the exercise of the legitimate rights to freedom and independence." Pursuant to Resolution 2165 (XXI) of December 5, 1966 the issue of military bases on foreign soil was referred to the UN Conference on Disarmament and was reaffirmed in Resolution 2344 (XXII) of December 19, 1967.

In this context, during the relevant discussions in the UN General Assembly and Security Council concerning the United States military presence in the Panama Canal Zone, the principles enunciated in the "Friendly Relations Resolution" of 1970 were reaffirmed and relied upon as constituting customary international law. It was thus argued that the old *Hay-Bunau-Varilla Treaty* between the United States and Panama had become obsolete by virtue of the emergence of a new international legal order based on the UN Charter.

With regard to military bases on foreign soil, the Belgrade Summit of the Non-Aligned Movement adopted a declaration, which refers to foreign military bases as a residue of colonialism and a violation of national sovereignty. Article 11 of the Declaration considers such bases to constitute a threat to international peace and security within the meaning of article 39 of the UN Charter. Every summit of the Non-Aligned Movement has demanded that foreign military bases be dismantled.

(iii) Implied Right of Denunciation

The majority of modern treaties contain provisions for termination or withdrawal. Sometimes it is provided that the treaty shall come to an end automatically after a certain time, or when a particular event occurs; other treaties merely give each party an option to withdraw, usually after giving a certain period of notice. Moreover, in the light of the fact that in international practice the longest-running leases are for 99 years, it would appear that after 119 years since the initial lease of 1903, the Guantánamo lease is overdue for termination. Even the *Hay-Bunau-Varilla Treaty*, which was not a mere lease, but actually granted sovereignty "in perpetuity" over the Panama Canal zone was subject to revision in 1977.

Finally, any good faith interpretation of the lease would have to focus on the language recognizing Cuban sovereignty over the territory. Article 31 VCLT stipulates: "A treaty shall be interpreted in good faith in accordance with the ordinary meaning to be given to the terms of the treaty in their context and in the light of its object and purpose." If "sovereignty" means anything, it means that the sovereign must retain some attributes of sovereignty, even if it temporarily gives up jurisdiction over a given territory. Thus, a sovereign must be able to regain the exercise of jurisdiction over the territory in question, otherwise it is not sovereign. The language of the Guantánamo lease does not indicate that Cuba ever intended or contemplated a cession of territory. Had cession or purchase been intended by the parties, they could have so provided in the text of the treaty. In this context, it should be recalled that the United States initially wanted to purchase the territory, as envisaged in article VII of the Platt Amendment, but that the Cuban negotiators limited the agreement to a "lease." Moreover, since the agreement speaks of Cuba's "continued ultimate sovereignty," this implies that it was envisaged by both parties that sooner or later the territory would revert to Cuba. A lease agreement is not the equivalent of a cession or a sale. A lease, which confers lesser rights than sovereignty, cannot be perpetual unless the sovereign agrees by a recognizable and unmistakable act.

(iv) Fundamental Change in Circumstances: clausula rebus sic stantibus

The fundamental change of circumstances, otherwise known as the *clausula rebus sic stantibus*, can also be invoked to test the validity of treaties dating back from colonial times. Newly independent nations have resorted to this argument in order to terminate their inherited burdens, sometimes with reference to article 62 VCLT. They have invoked the doctrine not only on the basis of justice but also because a treaty fails to accord with the present conditions of the world. Thus, it could be argued that the lease of a military base in a foreign country is conditioned on the friendly relations between those States, and that as alliance treaties are deemed to terminate when a new sovereign government is fundamentally opposed to the alliance, similarly the presence of a hostile nation on the sovereign territory of Cuba is contrary to modern conceptions of sovereignty and of the sovereign equality of States.

(v) Termination by Virtue of Material Breach of the Agreement

Pursuant to article 60 VCLT, a treaty is voidable by virtue of material breach of its provisions. According to the terms of articles 1 and 2 of the 1903 Lease Agreement, the use of the Guantánamo Bay territory was limited to coaling and naval purposes only, "and for no other purpose." It would follow that the repeated use of the territory as an internment camp (for 36,000 Haitian refugees in the years 1991 to 1994, and 21,000 Cuban refugees in the 1990s) or as a detention and interrogation centre and prisoner of war camp (where trials and even executions are envisaged) is wholly incompatible with the object and purpose of the treaty. This entails a material breach of the agreement, justifying unilateral termination by Cuba in accordance with article 60 VCLT.

Another serious concern is that of gross violations of international human rights norms and international humanitarian law occurring in the territory. According to five United Nations Rapporteurs, the International Committee of the Red Cross, Amnesty International and other observers, torture has been practiced in Guantánamo; this has been confirmed by a number of released detainees. These gross violations of human rights constitute an even graver breach of the Guantánamo lease agreement, justifying immediate termination.

As to the presence of a number of concessions and commercial enterprises in Guantánamo, including a McDonalds and a ten-pin bowling alley, it is certain that this constitutes a breach of the terms of article III of the supplemental Convention of July 2, 1903. However, since such a breach does not affect the object and purpose of the lease agreement and can be easily corrected by bilateral negotiation, it alone would not entail a material breach justifying termination of the lease.

CONCLUSION

There can be no doubt that under international law the Guantánamo lease agreement is voidable *ex nunc*. Cuba has no possibility to expel the United States from Guantánamo, as this would contravene the prohibition of the use of force contained in article 2(4) of the UN Charter and would furnish a pretext for a U.S. invasion. Cuba's persistent protests have the function of frustrating any eventual U.S. contention about putative Cuban acquiescence, thus preventing the U.S. from being able to claim sovereignty over the territory by virtue of occupation and prescription.

In the light of the international law obligation contained in article 2(3) of the UN Charter to settle disputes by peaceful means, the question of the continued validity of the lease could be tested by means of binding arbitration, or submission to adjudication by the International Court of Justice, if indeed the dispute cannot be settled through bi-lateral negotiation. Any such tribunal would have to interpret the meaning of the term "sovereignty," as it appears in article III of the 1903 Treaty. Yet another term requiring interpretation is the word "continued," since the agreement provides for Cuba's "continued ultimate sovereignty." The question arises whether "continued sovereignty" can be rendered meaningless by virtue of a lease agreement that does not state a specific date of termination. Moreover, in the light of the reality of de-colonization in Africa, Asia and Latin-America, considering the return to their sovereigns of leased territories such as Macau and Hong Kong, and bearing in mind the reversion of the Panama Canal to Panamanian sovereignty, it appears glaringly anachronistic that the "sovereign" in Guantánamo is unable to regain jurisdiction over its own territory, notwithstanding 63 years of consistent protests. The General Assembly could also submit this legal question to the International Court of Justice for an advisory opinion and also ask for a determination of an appropriate level of compensation for the use of Cuban territory for 124 years under neo-colonial conditions and for the ecological damage caused to the environment.

CASE STUDY: ELHAJ

As demonstrated in this chapter, the U.S. belligerent occupation of Guantánamo Bay since 1898 entails multiple violations of international law, including the UN Charter and pertinent General Assembly Resolutions concerning decolonization. Essentially,

Guantánamo Naval Base constitutes an anachronism, a vestige of U.S. imperialism, completely incompatible with principles of the sovereign equality of States and the self-determination of peoples, as well as the letter and spirt of the Charter.

The story of the Al Jazeera journalist Samy Elhaj is worth retelling. I met him in June 2008 at the offices of the United Nations High Commissioner for Refugees in Geneva and took the opportunity to interview him for the Swiss-German newspaper *Zeit-Fragen,* which is also published both on paper and online in a French language edition under the title "Horizons et Debats" and in English under the title "Current Concerns" (see pp. 130-31).

Samy was wrongly detained in Afghanistan, sent to Guantánamo and tortured for several years. His story is representative of the experience of hundreds of victims of the U.S. "War on Terror" and the criminal practice of "extraordinary rendition," both of which were condemned by Ben Emmerson, Q.C., the UN Rapporteur on Human Rights and Counter-Terrorism in his 2013 report to the UN Human Rights Council.

What is particularly relevant in the context of Cuban sovereignty over Guantánamo is not just that the "lease agreement" was forced upon Cuba in 1903 and denounced by Fidel Castro in 1959, but that Cuban sovereign territory (Article 1 of the lease agreement confirms that Cuba only gives jurisdiction to the U.S., stipulating that sovereignty remains with Cuba) was used for the commission of torture and other crimes, including indefinite detention of persons without due process, legal representation or contact with their families.[91] Such unconscionable abuse of the territory of Cuba by the U.S. justifies the immediate termination of the lease and the payment of appropriate reparations to Cuba for the gross violation of its sovereignty, and a claim for adequate compensation by the victims.

---

91 See my analysis, "Human rights and indefinite detention," in *International Review of the Red Cross,* 87:857 (March 2005), https://www.icrc.org/en/doc/assets/files/other/irrc_857_zayas.pdf

"We had no rights, we were not treated as human beings"*

Professor Alfred de Zayas: Mr. Elhaj, in May 2008 you were released from Guantánamo after more than six years detention. You are now in Geneva to meet with officials at the United Nations and the International Committee of the Red Cross. Back in December 2001 you were arrested on the border between Pakistan and Afghanistan. Although you had nothing to do with terrorism, you were not an "enemy combatant" and were never prosecuted, how do you explain your detention?

Sami Elhaj: The US military falsely alleged I was a courier for a militant Muslim organization. I am an Al-Jazeera journalist and was arrested probably because of US hostility toward Al-Jazeera and because the media was reporting on US rights violations in Afghanistan.

Have you demanded compensation from the US authorities for more than 6 years of arbitrary detention? Article 9(5) of the International Covenant on Civil and Political Rights stipulates a right of compensation in cases of arbitrary arrest or detention. Have you considered a class action of former Guantanamo detainees against the US for arbitrary detention, ill-treatment, torture, religious outrage, defamation?

I have come to Geneva so soon after my release because I am concerned about those who remain in Guantanamo Bay and who need my help. My focus right now is to increase awareness and understanding about the situation experienced by prisoners held in Guantanamo Bay where I was held, without charge, for 6 1/2 years. These men need to be released and many of them cannot return to their homes and need protection from other countries.

I also focus on increasing awareness regarding those thousands of prisoners still being detained in secret prisons around the world, including Iraq and Afghanistan, secret prisons that were established in the context of the 'war on terror'. There is also, of course, the need to consider the issue of moral and legal compensation for all those who have been victim to these measures and the torture and loss of dignity and freedom we have all suffered. Right now, I am focused on the release of the prisoners from these places of detention and for their human rights to be protected.

Are you writing a book about your experiences? – if not, why not?

I am working on many projects and I hope in the future to be able to record my experiences and thoughts in this way.

You have used a walking stick since your detention. Were you personally subjected to torture in Guantanamo?

Many, many things happened to me in the 6 1/2 years from the time when I was taken prisoner. These included being beaten. When I needed medical treatment due to a head injury caused by mistreatment, the doctor could only treat me through the bars of my cell. I was tied in difficult ways and kept in painful positions. I was kept in very cold cells and my clothes were taken from me as punishment. We were unable to keep track of the time, the days, the months. I went on a hunger strike to protest our situation and the way I was treated was inhumane and torturous. I was force-fed until I was sick, they used tubes which were unclean and very painful – many, many things. The way they treated the prisoners on hunger strike was a special kind of torture. We had no rights, we were not treated as human beings.

What was most difficult to endure in Guantanamo?

---

*Interview with Sami Elhaj, former Guantánamo inmate, conducted by Professor Alfred de Zayas, as it appeared in *Current Concerns* (2008, no. 7), p. 5. Also see https://www.rts.ch/info/monde/13173284-mohamedou-ould-slahi-en-quatorze-ans-je-nai-jamais-vu-le-soleil-se-lever-ou-se-coucher.html.

Mr. Elhaj, 38, now works as a producer for Qatar-based Al-Jazeera. He is the only journalist from a major international news organization to have been held at Guantanamo. (photo: AdZ)

The violation of dignity, the deprivation of contact with my family and the deprivation to be able to practice my faith.

Did you know the inmates who committed suicide?

I can say many things about this. First, I do not believe these inmates committed suicide and I have spoken to UN Human Rights officials about this during my trip to Geneva. I did know these men, and I know that one of them had even just recently received good news through his lawyer about his situation.

In the case of Ahmed Ali Abdullah, a Yemeni citizen, Alkarama/Dignity for Human Rights has helped the family organize an autopsy of their son's body. Alkarama commissioned a medical team headed by the director of the University of Lausanne's Institute of Forensic Medicine. The examination took place at the Sanaa Military Hospital. The autopsy report revealed a certain number of anomalies, in particular the American authorities' keeping anatomical organs corresponding to the upper airways, which constitute the centrepiece in a case of suicide by hanging. In the two other cases of the suspicious deaths of Yassir Talal az-Zahrani and Mani' Shaman al-Utaybi, these organs were also removed. The file on this issue is not yet closed.

Did you suffer religious insults or humiliation?

Yes, many times and I have seen many things. I have seen the Holy Koran stepped on with boots and insults and obscene phrases written on it. During questioning the interrogator sat on the Holy Koran and said he would not stand up until his questions were answered. They drew bad pictures of the Prophet Mohammed. They would cut our beards and take our clothes from us as punishment. They would pretend to be talking to Allah on the telephone, mocking him. They would force us to watch obscene and violent films and force us to describe what we had seen. Many, many things happened during all those years and it is a very painful matter. I was also subjected to racist comments – something I could not believe would happen in this century.

Thank you Mr. Elhaj for this interview, and may you be successful in facilitating the liberation of other innocent inmates in Guantanamo and elsewhere in the world. •

19.

Indiscriminate Bombardment of Population Centers: Reflections on Hiroshima and Nagasaki

War is always hell. The principal task of humanity must be to ensure prevention of armed conflict, and when there are international grievances, to facilitate negotiation and mediation. Once war starts, war crimes and crimes against humanity inevitably follow.

Peace can never come too soon, and all belligerents must be prepared to make concessions and refrain from making demands that will prolong the conflict and the suffering indefinitely. Among the criminal demands that have been made in past wars is that of "unconditional surrender" of the enemy, which essentially means the total dehumanization of the enemy, the reduction of the enemy to an infra-human status. One does not negotiate with infra-humans—one crushes them. Millions of lives have been lost to this particularly criminal concept: civilian populations in so many countries, victims of indiscriminate bombardment and fiery death; innocent women, men and children, terrorized by weapons of mass destruction, missiles, drones, shelling from armoured vehicles; traditional communities annihilated by the forces of hubris and hate; families buried under the roofs of their homes, dismembered, consumed in fire storms, scorched and disfigured by white phosphorus, napalm and agent orange; survivors deprived of water, food and shelter. . . . How many more orphans? How many more refugees?

On August 6, 1945 the city of Hiroshima served as a testing ground for a new, devastating weapon of mass destruction—the atomic bomb dropped by the *Enola Gay* B-29 under the command of Colonel Paul Tibbets upon the hapless Japanese population.

Unsuspecting human guinea pigs endured the first use of an atomic bomb on a population centre. It has been estimated that 140,000 human beings lost their lives in Hiroshima.[92] On August 8, 1945, the London Agreement establishing the statute of the Nuremberg tribunal was signed.

One day later, on August 9, a second indiscriminate attack on civilians took place. This time the women and children of Nagasaki were targeted for nuclear annihilation. It is estimated that 70,000 human beings perished in the inferno. How many human beings survived to carry the horror with them for the rest of their lives, the traumata, the cancers, the leukaemia, the pulmonary disorders, the multiple pathologies, the birth defects? How many generations have continued to suffer from the sequels of these unimaginable atrocities? What possible justification could be given for these mega-crimes?

Euphemisms are covers for genocide, for unspeakable crimes. Apologists have tried to minimize the enormity of the catastrophe, to justify the slaughter in terms of military necessity, of a lesser evil, of inducing a faster end to the war against Japan. What a profoundly immoral manipulation of reality! What a level of intellectual dishonesty! What cognitive depravity! What inversion of values!

---

92 International Committee of the Red Cross, "The Effects of Nuclear Weapons on Human Health," February 13, 2018, http://large.stanford.edu/courses/2018/ph241/kuppermann1/docs/icrc-feb13.pdf. According to Newsweek it is estimated that around 140,000 of Hiroshima's population of 350,000 were killed in the bombing, and it is estimated that around 74,000 people died in Nagasaki. In Hiroshima, on August 6, around 80,000 people were killed immediately when the bomb was dropped. In Nagasaki, on August 9, around 40,000 people were killed instantly. Tens of thousands of others died in the aftermath, of radiation poisoning and their injuries [Seren Morris, "How Many People Died in Hiroshima and Nagasaki?," *Newsweek,* August 3, 2020, https://www.newsweek.com/how-many-people-died-hiroshima-nagasaki-japan-second-world-war-1522276.] There are also higher estimates for Hiroshima. A 1998 study posited a figure of 202,118 registered deaths resulting from the Hiroshima bombing, a number that had swollen by 62,000 since the 1946 death toll of 140,000 [Henry Atkins, "How Many People Died in the Hiroshima and Nagasaki Bombings?" *HistoryHit,* August 9, 2018, https://www.historyhit.com/how-many-people-died-in-the-hiroshima-and-nagasaki-bombings/].

This brazen nonsense appeared in official communiqués, chauvinistic war literature, yellow journalism, and primitive propaganda. It routinely resurfaces in annual victory statements, in history textbooks that attempt to justify the massacres on theories of *Realpolitik*, on the oxymoron that unconditional surrender was the best means to achieve a clean sweep, a new start, a new world order. But what an order of consummate hypocrisy! What an apotheosis of power. What a display of the arrogant "might makes right" paradigm!

Let us recall the language of article 25 of the Regulations appended to Hague Convention IV of 1907:

> The attack or bombardment, by whatever means, of towns, villages, dwellings, or buildings which are undefended is prohibited.

Let us remember the preambular language of Hague Convention IV and the spirit of its famous "Martens Clause":

> Until a more complete code of the laws of war has been issued, the High Contracting Parties deem it expedient to declare that, in cases not included in the Regulations adopted by them, the inhabitants and the belligerents remain under the protection and the rule of the principles of the law of nations, as they result from the usages established among civilized peoples, from the laws of humanity, and the dictates of the public conscience.

In other words, the laws of war do not give warring parties a blank check and let them do anything they want. The principle of distinction between military and civilian objectives is paramount. The principle of proportionality is a corollary thereto. Indiscriminate weapons such as nuclear weapons are *by definition illegal* because they are indiscriminate and grossly violate the rule of proportionality. Collective punishment is in itself a crime against humanity.

Amazingly enough, many politicians in the 21st century continue to give lip service to these principles of law and justice. They sign and ratify conventions—and then violate them with impunity. Sometimes they make the effort to formulate exceptions, to look for loopholes in international humanitarian law, so that they can engage in carnage *ad libitum*, carnage *ad nauseam*, carnage à la carte.

The intellectual gymnastics that allowed the meta-crimes of Hiroshima and Nagasaki have survived to our generation. We have been taught to believe that the end justifies the means—and to disregard the obvious—to forget that it is the other way around. The use of criminal means always vitiates the end, which becomes an abomination against men and God.

Today victors continue wars by the instrumentalization of penal law for political and propagandistic purposes. They use thereby the pretext of combating impunity. But they intend to prosecute exclusively the crimes of the vanquished—*Vae victis*. By such a definition, the actions of the victorious power cannot be crimes. They may entail errors or judgment or unfortunate miscalculations—but not violations of legal principles.

What an irony of history that two days after the destruction of Hiroshima and one day before the destruction of Nagasaki the Allies adopted the Charter of the International Criminal Tribunal for the Nuremberg Trials, article 6(c) of which defines crimes against humanity as follows: "murder, extermination, enslavement, deportation, and other inhumane acts committed against any civilian population. . . . "

In February 2003, just before the U.S. invasion of Iraq, Nelson Mandela condemned the crimes committed by the United States over many decades. At 85 years of age, Mandela unleashed a scathing critique of the United States' decision to drop the atomic bombs on Hiroshima and Nagasaki:

"57 years ago, when Japan was retreating on all fronts,
they (U.S.) decided to drop the atom bomb in Hiroshima

and Nagasaki. Killed a lot of innocent people, who are still suffering from the effects of those bombs. Those bombs were not aimed against the Japanese. They were aimed against the Soviet Union. To say, look, this is the power that we have. If you dare oppose what we do, this is what is going to happen to you. Because they are so arrogant they decided to kill innocent people in Japan who are still suffering from that." Turning to U.S. unilateralism and President George W. Bush's plan to attack Iraq to remove Saddam Hussein, Mandela asked, "Who are they now to pretend that they are the policemen of the world?"[93]

All of these facts are in the public domain. Everyone can have access to some of these facts and a variety of interpretations thereof. This should trigger in their minds some doubts about past and future governmental explanations and narratives, questions about euphemisms, discernment between what is apparent and what is true, serene evaluation of past and current events and cautions projection of consequences and implications.

It is time to unlearn the lessons we were taught in politically approved treatises, in *Zeitgeist* history textbooks, in teleological political commentaries. It is time to call a spade a spade and recognize that pulverizing a population is nothing but State terrorism, unworthy of any government that pretends to adhere to principles of justice and the rule of law. It is time to recognize

---

93 "Nelson Mandela Condemns George W. Bush and War With Iraq, January 30th, 2003," YouTube video posted on Michael Moore channel, 03:48, https://www.youtube.com/watch?v=NQyN4X0sFdA; Luke Johnson, "Nelson Mandela Delivered One Of The Most Scathing Critiques Of Invading Iraq," *HuffPost*, December 5, 2013, updated January 25, 2014, https://www.huffpost.com/entry/nelson-mandela-iraq_n_4399015; "Nelson Mandela On US Imperialism Since Hiroshim," *Defend Democracy Press*, June 2, 2021, http://www.defenddemocracy.press/nelson-mandela-on-us-imperialism-since-hiroshima/; Vincent J. Intondi, "Nelson Mandela and the Bomb," *HuffPost*, December 9, 2013, updated February 8, 2014, https://www.huffpost.com/entry/nelson-mandela-and-the-bo_b_4407788.

that a demand for unconditional surrender is incompatible with the Marten's Clause, with international humanitarian law, with the very concept of civilization. The demand for unconditional surrender and the measures used to enforce it constitute a poor cover for the intent to commit genocide as defined in Article 2 of the 1948 Genocide Convention.

Wars must be ended as soon as possible, by negotiation and compromise. The ideas of total war and total victory have been discarded by international law. It is no longer possible to impose a Carthaginian "peace" on an adversary. This would necessarily entail crimes against humanity within the meaning of article 7 of the 1998 Rome Statute of the International Criminal Court.

A war that ends by mass murder of civilians destroys any possible justification that might have been sought from the ritual invocation of the much abused "just war" doctrine. It makes a farce out of war crimes trials. It becomes an aberration in itself.

Euphemisms like "collateral damage" are constructed to hide the horror of slaughtering innocent civilians, women and children. Euphemisms are a form of self-deception intended to assuage the guilty consciences of political leaders and to keep a democratic public from standing up and demanding accountability, saying unequivocally "Not in our names."

The history of wars abundantly illustrates the use and abuse of slogans. In our lifetime we all have been subjected to too many slogans, including "my country right or wrong." which would apparently give justification to any abomination. This is not patriotism—this is stupidity.

Another maxim from which we often seek consolation is: "The truth will make you free." But unless that truth leads to action, it will remain an empty promise. *If* we presuppose that truth will come like a white knight to deliver us, that an outside force will solve our problems, that a *Deus in machina* will ensure a happy end. No. It is up to us to proactively seek truth, disseminate truth, liberate the word, use truth as a sword to cut through pretence and manipulation. Truth will reveal the degree of control to which we are all subject, the brainwashing, the robotization of our lives. Truth will enable us to develop a survival strategy and targeted tactics to counter Big Brother, refute political lies and expose opportunism. Truth will help us understand our common humanity and the necessity to live together in peace.

The United States did have a President who understood the big picture. At his farewell address in January 1981 Jimmy Carter said:

> It's now been 35 years since the first atomic bomb fell on Hiroshima. The great majority of the world's people cannot remember a time when the nuclear shadow did not hang over the Earth. Our minds have adjusted to it, as after a time our eyes adjust to the dark. Yet the risk of a nuclear conflagration has not lessened. It has not happened yet, thank God, but that can give us little comfort, for it only has to happen once.
>
> The danger is becoming greater. As the arsenals of the superpowers grow in size and sophistication and as other governments, perhaps even in the future dozens of governments, acquire these weapons, it may only be a matter of time before madness, desperation, greed, or miscalculation lets loose this terrible force.
>
> In an all-out nuclear war, more destructive power than in all of World War II would be unleashed every second during the long afternoon it would take for all the missiles and bombs to fall. A World War II every second—more people killed in the first few hours than in all the wars of history put together. The survivors, if any, would live in despair amid the poisoned ruins of a civilization that had committed suicide."[94]

---

94 Jimmy Carter, "Farewell Address to the Nation," January 14, 1981, *The American Presidency Project*, https://www.presidency.ucsb.edu/documents/farewell-address-the-nation-0

The Nobel Peace Prize 2017 was awarded to the International Campaign to Abolish Nuclear Weapons[95]

"for its work to draw attention to the catastrophic humanitarian consequences of any use of nuclear weapons and for its ground-breaking efforts to achieve a treaty-based prohibition of such weapons."

Ultimately, the right to life is the alpha and omega of human rights. The right to life necessarily entails the recognition that Peace is a human right, a recognition that the General Assembly has not yet given. We urgently need a change of mindset. Civil society activists gave birth to the Declaración de Santiago de Compostela of December 10, 2010. They also campaigned for a Treaty for the Abolition of Nuclear Weapons.[96]

This Treaty is the best hope for humanity. It was adopted by the General Assembly on July 7, 2017, opened for signature on September 20, 2017, and entered into force on January 22, 2021.

Their acceptance speech in Oslo was delivered by Setsuko Thurlow, a Hiroshima survivor, who said:[97]

I speak as a member of the family of hibakusha – those of us who, by some miraculous chance, survived the atomic bombings of Hiroshima and Nagasaki. For more than seven decades, we have worked for the total abolition of nuclear weapons.

---

95 See International Campaign to Abolish Nuclear Weapons (ICAN), https://www.icanw.org/ and The Nobel Prize, "International Campaign to Abolish Nuclear Weapons Facts," https://www.nobelprize.org/prizes/peace/2017/ican/facts/.

96 UN Office for Disarmament Affairs, "Treaty on the prohibition of nuclear weapons," https://www.un.org/disarmament/wmd/nuclear/tpnw/.

97 The Nobel Prize, "International Campaign to Abolish Nuclear Weapons Nobel Lecture," https://www.nobelprize.org/prizes/peace/2017/ican/lecture/.

We have stood in solidarity with those harmed by the production and testing of these horrific weapons around the world. People from places with long-forgotten names, like Moruroa, Ekker, Semipalatinsk, Maralinga, Bikini. People whose lands and seas were irradiated, whose bodies were experimented upon, whose cultures were forever disrupted.

We were not content to be victims. We refused to wait for an immediate fiery end or the slow poisoning of our world. We refused to sit idly in terror as the so-called great powers took us past nuclear dusk and brought us recklessly close to nuclear midnight. We rose up. We shared our stories of survival. We said: humanity and nuclear weapons cannot coexist....

Tonight, as we march through the streets of Oslo with torches aflame, let us follow each other out of the dark night of nuclear terror. No matter what obstacles we face, we will keep moving and keep pushing and keep sharing this light with others. This is our passion and commitment for our one precious world to survive.

THE
UKRAINE WAR:
CAUSES AND
IMPLICATIONS

20.

A Culture of Cheating

The current tensions between the United States and Russia with regard to Ukraine goes back to a series of NATO actions and omissions following the demise of the Soviet Union in 1989/91. On the Russian side there is a widespread perception of having been misled by the U.S. and NATO, a pervasive malaise about a breach of trust, a violation of a "gentleman's agreement" on fundamental issues of national security.

While the U.S. protests that it never gave assurances to Gorbachev that NATO would not expand eastwards, declassified documents have emerged to prove otherwise. But even in the absence of declassified documents and contemporary statements by political leaders in 1989/91 including those by Secretary of State James Baker and German Foreign Minister Hans-Dietrich Genscher (which can be verified in YouTube), it is all-too-obvious that there is a festering wound caused by NATO's eastward expansion over the past 30 years, which undoubtedly has negatively impacted Russia's sense of security. No country likes to be encircled by a country whose aims it distrusts, and common sense should tell Americans that maybe we should not be provoking another nuclear power. At the very least, NATO's provocations are unwise, at worst they could spell Apocalypse.

We in the West play innocent, and retreat into legal "positivism," asserting that there was no signed treaty commitment, that the assurances were not written in stone. Yet, *Realpolitik* tells us that if one side breaks its word, or is perceived as having double-crossed the other side, if it acts in a manner contrary to the spirit of an agreement and to the overriding principle of good faith (*bona fide*), there are political consequences.

It seems, however, that we in the West have gotten so used to what I term a "culture of cheating," that we display surprise when another country does not simply accept the fact that we cheated them in the past, and that notwithstanding this breach of trust, they should accept the "new normal" and resume "business as usual." as if that had not happened. The West's leaders in the U.S., UK, EU contend that they have a clean conscience and refuse to consider the fact that the other side has issues about having been taken for a ride. A rational person, *a fortiori* a statesman, would pause and try to defuse the "misunderstanding." Yet, the U.S. culture of cheating has become so second nature to Americans, that we do not even realize it when we are cheating someone else and seem incapable of understanding that going on to deny our actions and renege on our words adds insult to injury.

The culture of cheating is family to the doctrine of "exceptionalism." We self-righteously claim the right to cheat others, but others cannot cheat us. *Quod licet Iovi non licet bovi* (that which Jupiter can do is not permitted for the bovines). This constitutes a kind of predator behavior that neither religion nor civilization has succeeded in eradicating. We mount false-flag operations and accuse the other side of the same. The CIA and M15 have been caught red handed on so many occasions—and yet no one seems to be asking whether, in the long run, such behavior is not counter-productive, whether our credibility is shot. And what that will mean, if it is.

Perhaps one explanation for this kind of behavior is that we have elevated the culture of cheating to a kind of secular virtue—equivalent to cunning, daring and boldness. It is seen as a positive attribute when a leader is "craftier" and "sneakier" than his/her rival. The name of the game is to score points in an atmosphere of perpetual competition, where there are no rules. Our geopolitical competitors are just that—rivals—and there is no interest whatever in fraternizing with adversaries. Cooperation is somehow perceived as "weak," as "Un-American." "Dirty tricks" are not seen as dishonest, but as clever, even patriotic, because they are intended to advance the economic and political interests of our country. Paradoxically, "dirty tricks" are perceived in a positive light as artful, ingenious, adventurous, even visionary. This curious approach to reality is facilitated by a compliant and complicit corporate media that does not call out the liars' bluffs and instead disseminates "fake news" and suppresses dissenting views. Unless one has the presence of mind and capacity to do one's own research and to access other sources of information, one is caught in the propaganda web.

The U.S. government has practiced this culture of cheating in its international relations for more than two hundred years, particularly in its dealings with the First Nations of the continent, who again and again were lied to, and whose lands and resources were shamelessly stolen. As Martin Luther King Jr. wrote in his book *Why We Can't Wait:* "Our nation was born in genocide" (p. 120). How many "Indian" Treaties were broken, again and again? And when the Sioux, Cree and Navajo protested, we massacred them. See the studies of the UN Sub-Commission on Promotion and Protection of Human Rights.[98]

This "culture of cheating" can be documented countless times in connection with the Monroe Doctrine and U.S. relations with Mexico, Latin America, Hawaii, the Philippines, etc.

One of the elements that is totally missing from the current Ukraine debate is the right of self-determination of peoples.

---

98 "Reassessing the paradigm of domestication: the problematic of indigenous treaties," *The Free Library,* https://www.thefreelibrary.com/Reassessing+the+paradi gm+of+domestication%3a+the+problematic+of...-a0238269291 (accessed May 24, 2022). See also UN Office of the High Commissioner of Human Rights press releases: "Subcommission Continues Discussion of Rights of Indigenous Peoples," Aug. 17, 1999, https://www.ohchr.org/en/press-releases/2009/10/subcommission-continues-discussion-rights-indigenous-peoples; and "Commission Adopts Texts on Indigenous Issues, Report of Sub-Commission, Promotion, and Protection of Human Rights," April 20, 2005, https://www.ohchr.org/en/press-releases/2009/10/commission-adopts-texts-indigenous-issues-report-sub-commission-promotion; and the *Universal Periodic Review on Canada* joint submission by Samson Cree Nation, Ermineskin Cree Nation, Louis Bull Tribe, Montana Cree Nation, and International Organization of Indigenous Resource Development to the UN Human Rights Council, September 2008, https://lib.ohchr.org/HRBodies/UPR/Documents/Session4/CA/JS2_CAN_UPR_S4_2009_InternationalOrganizationofIndigenousResourceDevelopment_etal_JOINT.pdf.

Undoubtedly the Russians in the Ukraine are not just a minority but constitute a "people"—and as such the Russians in Donetsk, Lugansk and Crimea possess the right of self-determination. enshrined in the UN Charter and in Article 1 common to the International Covenant on Civil and Political Rights (ICCPR) and Covenant on Economic, Social and Cultural Rights. Back in March and June 1994 I monitored the parliamentary and presidential elections in the Ukraine as representative of the UN Secretary General. I travelled around the country. No doubt that the Russian-speakers had a profound sense of Russian identity. Until the Western-engineered, deliberately anti-Russian *coup d'état* of February 2014, the Ukrainians and Russian-Ukrainians had lived side by side in relative harmony. Maidan brought with it Russophobic elements that have since been exacerbated by a systematic war propaganda and incitement to hatred by the Ukrainian government and Western NGOs, both prohibited by article 20 of the ICCPR. Thus, in view of recent events, it is unlikely that the Russians in the Donbass will ever feel safe enough to want to continue living with Ukrainians who have been and are being incited not just to hatred but to actual military attacks against them.

There would be no conflict in Ukraine today if Barack Obama, Victoria Nuland and several European leaders had not destabilized the democratically elected government of Viktor Yanukovych and organized a vulgar *coup d'état* to install Western puppets. Bottom line: Western interference in the internal affairs of other States can backfire, and the culture of cheating and deceit that we continue to practice renders it impossible to reach sustainable solutions.

21.

NATO: The Belief System of "The Good Guys"

The U.S./NATO/Ukraine/Russia controversy is not entirely new. We already saw the potential of serious trouble in 2014 when the U.S. and European states interfered in the internal affairs of Ukraine and covertly/overtly colluded in the *coup d'état* against the democratically elected President of Ukraine, Viktor Yanukovych, because he was not playing the game assigned to him by the West. Of course, our media hailed the putsch as a "color revolution" with all the trappings of democracy.

The 2021/22 Russia-Ukraine crisis is a logical continuation of the expansionist policies that NATO has pursued since the demise of the Soviet Union, as numerous esteemed professors of international law and international relations have long indicated—including Richard Falk, John Mearsheimer, Stephen Kinzer and Francis Boyle. NATO's approach implements the U.S. claim to have a "mission" to export its socio-economic model to other countries, notwithstanding the preferences of these sovereign states and the right of self-determination of peoples.

Although the U.S. and NATO narratives have been proven to be inaccurate and sometimes deliberately mendacious on numerous occasions, it remains the fact that a majority of citizens in the Western World uncritically believe what they are told. The "quality press" including *The New York Times*, *Washington Post*, *The Times*, *Le Monde*, *El Pais*, the German *NZZ* and *FAZ* are all effective echo chambers of the Washington consensus and enthusiastically support the public relations and geopolitical propaganda offensive.

I think that it can be said without fear of contradiction that the only war that NATO has ever won is the information war. A compliant and complicit corporate media has been successful in persuading millions of Americans and Europeans that the toxic narratives of the Ministries of Foreign Affairs are really true. We believe in the myth of the "Arab Spring" and "EuroMaidan," but we never hear about the right of self-determination of peoples, including the Russians of Donetsk and Lugansk, and what could easily be called the "Crimean Spring."

Often, I ask myself how this is possible when it is pretty widely known that the U.S. deliberately lied in earlier conflicts in order to make aggression appear as "defense." We were lied to in connection with the "Gulf of Tonkin" incident in Vietnam, the alleged weapons of mass destruction in Iraq. There is abundant evidence that the CIA and M15 have organized "false flag" events throughout the Middle East and elsewhere. Why is it that masses of educated people fail to take some distance from the lies and question more? I dare postulate the hypothesis that the best way to understand the NATO phenomenon is to see it as a secular religion: the belief system of "the good guys." If so viewed, then we can allow ourselves to believe its implausible narratives. They have to be true: after all, *we are the good guys.*

NATO's implicit credo is somewhat Calvinistic—it's a credo for and by the "elect." And by definition, we in the West are the "elect." Only we shall have salvation, only we grasp the truth—which can all be taken on faith. As every religion, the NATO religion has its own dogma and lexicon. In NATO's lexicon democracy is co-terminous with capitalism, humanitarian intervention entails "regime change." "rule of law" means OUR rules, "Satan No. 1" is Putin, and Satan No. 2 is Xi Jinping.

Of course, NATO is hardly a religion of *Beatitudes* and Sermon on the Mount (Matthew V, 3–10), except for one typically Western Beatitude—*Beati possidetis*—blessed are those who possess and occupy. What's mine is mine, what's yours is negotiable. What I occupy, I stole it fair and square. When we look at NATO as a religion, we can better understand certain political developments in Europe and the Middle East, Ukraine, Yugoslavia, Libya, Syria, Iraq.

Worse than garden variety absurdity—the maintenance of our belief in NATO necessitates constant and ongoing broad spectrum lying to the American people, to the UN, to the world. The WMD propaganda concoction in 2003 was not just a simple "*pia fraus*"—or white lie. It was well orchestrated and there were many players.

A million Iraqis paid with their lives and their country was devastated. As an American, I and an estimated 10 million others worldwide protested. But who listened? UN Secretary General Kofi Annan repeatedly called the invasion contrary to the UN Charter, and when cornered by journalists for clarification, he at last affirmed outright that the invasion was "an illegal war." Worse than being merely an illegal war, it was the most serious violation of the Nuremberg Principles since the Nuremberg Trials—a veritable revolt against international law. Not only the U.S. but the so-called "coalition of the willing," 43 States ostensibly legally committed to the UN Charter and to the International Covenant on Civil and Political Rights, deliberately assaulted the international rule of law.

One would think that after one has been lied to in matters of life and death, a healthy scepticism, some degree of caution, would set in, that rational people would think "haven't we heard this kind of propaganda before?" But no, if NATO is indeed a religion, we *a priori* take its pronouncements on faith. We do not question Jens Stoltenberg. There seems to be a tacit agreement that lying in matters of state is "honorable" and that questioning it is "unpatriotic"—again the Machiavellian principle that the supposedly good end justifies the evil means.

Apostasy is one of the problems with any religion. This happens often when the leaders of a religion brazenly lie to the faithful. When people lose faith in the present leadership, they look for something else to believe in, e.g. history, heritage, tradition. I dare consider myself a U.S. patriot—and yet also an apostate from the NATO religion—because I reject the idea "my country right or wrong." I want my country to be right and to do justice—and when the country is on the wrong track, I want it to return to the ideals of the Constitution, of our Declaration of Independence, of the Gettysburg address—something I can still believe in.

NATO has emerged as the perfect religion for bullies and warmongers, not unlike other expansive ideologies of the past. The Romans were proud of their legions, the French grenadiers gladly died for Napoleon's glories, GIs by the thousands applauded the bombing campaigns over Vietnam, Laos, and Cambodia.

Personally, I view NATO in the tradition of the village bully. But emotionally most Americans do not have the temerity to reject our leadership. Perhaps because NATO auto-proclaims itself to be a positive force for democracy and human rights, and to do so would put themselves in the position of questioning what is widely taken to be good.

Many religions are solipsistic, self-aggrandizing, based on the premise that they and they alone possess the truth—and that whatever is threatening that truth—*the devil*—represents unspeakable evil. NATO fits right in with this scenario, as a classical solipsist faith-based structure, self-contained, self-serving, based on the premise that NATO is by definition the force for good. A solipsist (or egotist) is incapable of self-reflection, self-criticism, incapable to see others on a par with himself—with strengths and frailties, and possibly with some inconvenient truths as well.

NATO builds on the "exceptionalist" dogma that has been developed and practiced by the United States for more than two centuries. Pursuant to the doctrine of "exceptionalism," the U.S. and NATO are both above international law—even above natural law. "Exceptionalism" is another expression for the Roman slogan *"quod licet Jovi, non licet bovi"*—that which Jupiter can do—is certainly not allowed for common mortals like us—We are the "Bovi," the bovines.

Moreover, we in the West have become so used to our "culture of cheating"—that we react surprised when another country does not simply accept that we cheated them. This culture of cheating has become so second nature to us, that we do not even realize it when we cheat someone else. This is a form of predator behavior that civilization has not succeeded yet in eradicating.

Might NATO rather be seen as a reflection of 21st century imperialism, akin to neo-colonialism but with this difference: NATO not only provokes and threatens geopolitical rivals, it actually loots and exploits its own member States—not for their own security—but for the benefit of the military-industrial complex. It should seem obvious to everyone—but it doesn't—that Europe's security lies in dialogue and compromise, in understanding the views of all human beings living in the continent. Security was never identical with the arms race, sabre-rattling and expansionism.

According to the mainstream narrative, the crimes committed by NATO over the past 73 years are not crimes but regrettable errors by an entity that means well. As a historian—not only a jurist—I acknowledge that we may be losing the battle for truth. It is quite possible—and horrific—that in thirty, fifty, eighty years, NATO's propaganda will emerge as the accepted historical truth, solidly cemented and repeated in history books. This is partly because most historians, like lawyers, are pens for hire. Forget about the illusion that as time passes historical objectivity increases. On the contrary, all the canards that eyewitnesses can debunk today ultimately become the accepted historical narrative once the experts are all dead and can no longer challenge the narrative. Forget declassified documents that contradict the narrative, because experience shows that only very seldom can they overthrow a well-entrenched political lie. Indeed, the political lie will not die until it has ceased to be politically useful.

Unfortunately, many Americans and Europeans continue to buy the NATO narrative—perhaps because it is easy and comforting to think that we are the "good guys" and that the grave dangers "out there" make NATO necessary for our survival. As Julius Caesar wrote in his "*De bello civile*"—*quae volumus, ea credimus libenter.* What we want to believe, we believe—in other words, *mundus vult decipi*—the world actually wants to be deceived

Objectively seen, NATO's expansion and non-stop provocation of Russia was and is a dangerous geopolitical error, a betrayal of the trust owed by us to the Russian people—worse yet—a betrayal of the hope for peace shared by the great majority of humanity. In 1989/91 we had the opportunity and the responsibility to guarantee global peace. Hubris and megalomania killed that hope. The military-industrial-financial complex relies on perpetual war to continue making billions of dollars in profits. The demise of the Soviet Union could have ushered in an era of UN Charter implementation, of respect for international law, a serious effort to at least begin to convert military-first economies into human security and human services economies, a slashing of useless military budgets with the direction of the liberated funds into eradicating poverty, malaria, pandemics, research and development in the health sector, improving hospitals and infrastructure, addressing climate change, maintaining roads and bridges . . . .

Who bears the responsibility for this massive betrayal of the world? The late President George H.W. Bush and the late British Prime Minister Margaret Thatcher, together with their successors and all their neo-con advisors and proponents of "exceptionalism," together with the think tanks and pundits that cheered them on.

How was this betrayal possible? Only through disinformation and propaganda. In fact, through the outright lies of a purported "mushroom cloud." Only with the complicity of the corporate media, which post the collapse of the Soviet Union applauded Fukuyama's idea of "the end of history" and "winner takes all." For a brief period, the U.S. revelled in the illusion of being the only hegemon. How long did this chimera of the unipolar world last? And how many atrocities were committed by NATO to impose its hegemony on the world—how many crimes against humanity were committed in the name of "democracy" and "European values"?

The corporate media dutifully played the game by declaring Russia and China to be our sworn enemies. Any reasonable discussion with the Russians and Chinese was and is decried as "appeasement." But shouldn't we look in the mirror and acknowledge that the only ones who require "appeasement" is us—and we accept no such thing?

If there is a country that cares precious little for the international rule of law—otherwise known as Blinken's "rules-based international order"—it is, alas, my country, the United States of America.

Among the international treaties that the U.S. has failed to ratify are the Vienna Convention on the Law of Treaties, the ICC Statute, The UN Convention on the Law of the Sea, the Open Skies Treaty, the Optional Protocol to the Vienna Convention on Diplomatic Relations, the Optional Protocol to the Vienna Convention on Consular Relations, the UN Convention on the Rights of the Child, the Convention on Migrant Workers, the Convention on Economic, Social and Cultural Rights. . . .

At the end of the day, we understand that neither Samuel Huntington nor Francis Fukuyama got the 21st century right—George Orwell did.

22.

Blueprints for Peace

As a peace activist for the past fifty years, I had the opportunity to participate in the drafting of the most promising civil society initiative for peace—the 2010 *Declaración de Santiago de Compostela*[99] (see below chapter 30)—and the subsequent draft text of the UN Declaration on the Right to Peace established by the Advisory Committee of the Human Rights Council.[100]

This excellent text was systematically sabotaged by the U.S. and the European countries who adamantly rejected the existence of a right to peace.[101] I participated as an expert in all consultations of the open-ended inter-governmental working group on the right to peace 2013–16, both in my capacity as UN Independent Expert[102] and as an NGO representative. Those who attended these consultations went away with the impression that the "West" remains committed to a war logic and is unwilling to surrender their "might makes right" doctrine and the full-spectrum dominance mindset, which they have so unremittingly employed.

This and other similar consultations are very revealing when it comes to understanding which countries actually support the philosophy of human rights, and which countries just master the jargon and give lip service to "values." It was clear that the interests of the military-industrial-financial complex had to be

---

99 El Congreso Internacional sobre el Derecho Humano a la Paz, *Declaración de Santiago Sobre El Derecho Humano a la Paz,* December 10, 2010, http://www.aedidh.org/sites/default/files/DS%20pdf%2024%20marzo%202011.pdf

100 Report of the Human Rights Council Advisory Committee on the right of peoples to peace, A/HRC/20/31, https://www.ohchr.org/en/hr-bodies/hrc/advisory-committee/right-to-peace

101 A/HRC/17/39/Corr.1.

102 UN Human Rights, Office of the High Commissioner, "The right to peace," April 4, 2013, https://www.ohchr.org/en/stories/2013/04/right-peace

defended. No western country endorsed a commitment to end the arms race or present a plan of action to achieve disarmament for development and for an end to the arms race.

The result was the watered-down resolution adopted by the 71st session of the UN General Assembly,[103] a significant retrogression from GA Resolution 39/11 of November 19, 1984.[104] In chapter 3 of my book *Building a Just World Order*[105] I describe a number of other peace initiatives. As a retired UN independent expert, I have also been asked to brainstorm and contribute to several peace models for Europe, the Ukraine and Russia.

It is obvious that any sustainable peace settlement must be based on a *quid pro quo* and must be compatible with the UN Charter, recognize the right of self- determination of all peoples of the world, including the Russians of Crimea and Donbass, and adopt a global security architecture that will protect the rights of all states. A peace settlement based on the principle "winner takes all," would only be a short-lived arrangement. In a world of nuclear weapons, everything must be done to achieve nuclear disarmament.

A global conference on peace and disarmament is urgently needed and should be convoked by the United Nations. Concrete agreements on disarmament for development should be drafted, equipped with implementation mechanisms and monitoring "observatories." The UN should also organize and monitor referenda in all conflict areas in the world, bearing in mind that it is not the *jus cogens* right of all peoples to self-determination that leads to war, but the unjust denial thereof. The UN must finally

---

103 "Declaration on the Right to Peace: resolution / adopted by the General Assembly," *United Nations Digital Library,* https://digitallibrary.un.org/record/858594.

104 "Declaration on the Right of Peoples to Peace," adopted November 12, 1984, by General Assembly resolution 39/11, https://www.ohchr.org/en/instruments-mechanisms/instruments/declaration-right-peoples-peace

105 Alfred de Zayas, *Building a Just World Order* (Atlanta, Ga.: Clarity Press, 2021), https://www.claritypress.com/product/building-a-just-world-order/

acknowledge that the realization of the right of self-determination constitutes an effective conflict-prevention strategy.

The International Progress Organization,[106] an Austrian
think tank with headquarters in Vienna, is devoted to world
peace and international solidarity. IPO has been dealing with a
whole spectrum of world affairs since the 1970s,[107] and conducts
international monitoring and observer missions.[108] It is active in
the United Nations, where it enjoys consultative status with the
Economic and Social Council. Its principal aim is to promote
peaceful co-existence among nations, further dialogue and cultural exchange among civilizations in the spirit of the UNESCO
Constitution.[109]

Among its publications are essays on a just international
economic order, global respect for human rights and the rule
of law.[110] With members in more than 70 countries on all five
continents, it convenes conferences, consultations and expert
meetings on issues of international law, conflict resolution, civi-
lizational dialogue, and United Nations reform. Since 1978 IPO
has published the series *Studies in International Relations* as well
as monographs in the field of international relations theory. Its
current president is Professor Hans Koechler[111] of the University
of Innsbruck.

The IPO Blueprint for Peace reproduced below was
endorsed by many professors of international law, including
myself.

---

106 International Progress Organization (IPO), https://i-p-o.org/.

107 IPO Declaration of the First General Assembly, https://i-p-o.org/ipodecl.
htm.

108 IPO International monitoring and observer missions, https://i-p-o.org/ipo_
int_monitoring.htm.

109 Meguro UNESCO Association, https://meguro-unesco.info/english/
constitution.html.

110 IPO publications on democracy in the international context, https://i-p-o.
org/int-dem.htm

111 Hans Köchler online: http://hanskoechler.com/.

BLUEPRINT FOR PEACE

In the present state of armed conflict between Russia and Ukraine, peaceful co-existence can only be restored, and sustained, on the basis of respect for international law and by way of political compromise between both parties. The former includes the non-use of force and respect for sovereignty and territorial integrity of Ukraine, as affirmed by an overwhelming majority of United Nations member states in General Assembly resolution ES-11/1 of 2 March 2022, adopted under the provisions of the "Uniting for peace" resolution of 3 November 1950. The latter relates to previous understandings and agreements reached between the conflicting parties and to the consensus on a European security architecture since the Helsinki Final Act of 1975.

The indivisibility of security in Europe, solemnly emphasized by the 1975 Conference on Security and Co-operation in Europe (CSCE) and reaffirmed in the Charter of Paris for a New Europe (1990), should be the guiding principle for the way forward. The Istanbul Document 1999 ("Charter for European Security"), adopted within the framework of the OSCE (Organization for Security and Co-operation in Europe) and signed by both conflicting parties, similarly confirmed, in Article 8, the "equal right to security" of all European states and stipulated that States "will not strengthen their security at the expense of the security of other States."

Taking into account that Ukraine is a multi-ethnic state, with ethnic Russians forming the largest minority, the following measures appear conducive to a peaceful settlement:

- Full implementation of the Minsk agreements according to the "Package of Measures" agreed between both parties—in the framework of the "Trilateral Contact Group" including the OSCE—on 12 February 2015. This includes in particular the stipulation of Article

11 for constitutional reform in Ukraine to provide for decentralization and an autonomous status of Russian majority areas in the eastern region (Donetsk and Lugansk). The compromise ("Südtirol-Paket") reached between Austria and Italy on autonomy of the province of South Tyrol, inhabited by a German-speaking majority, could serve as an example.

- A popular referendum under the auspices of the United Nations and/or the OSCE in the area of the Crimean peninsula on the final status of the territory.

- Adoption by the Ukrainian Parliament of a constitutional law on the permanent neutrality of Ukraine in connection with international guarantees of the country's sovereignty and territorial integrity (similar to the arrangements in the cases of Austria, after World War II, and Switzerland, after the Napoleonic wars). As in the cases of Austria and Switzerland, Ukraine's status should be one of armed neutrality so that the country will remain able to defend itself.

- Ukraine's commitment to a nuclear free status, enshrined in the Budapest Memorandum of 5 December 1994, should—in tandem with a future commitment to permanent neutrality—be accompanied by credible security guarantees (not mere "assurances"), with precise implementation mechanisms, on the part of the international community. In that regard, the Budapest Memorandum should be superseded by a new international agreement between Ukraine and the permanent members of the UN Security Council (P5) + Turkey, as regional mediating power, to be ratified by all signatory states.

- Withdrawal of all foreign troops from Ukrainian territory must go in tandem with the total lifting of unilateral sanctions against Russia.

This blueprint is moderate and realistic. But there can be no peace agreement for as long as one party is unwilling to compromise, for as long as one party continues to change its position. There are abundant reports that the Ukrainian President Zelinsky has been under considerable pressure from Washington and Brussels not to make peace but to continue fighting in the expectation of "winning" against Russia. Any reasonable person would realize that this is an impossible undertaking and that the United States and NATO are fighting a proxy war against Russia in the Ukraine, a war that they are prepared to fight until the last Ukrainian. There is zero desire for peace on the part of Washington and Brussels, partly because the military-industrial complex is making enormous profits out of this war.

Another association which is genuinely committed to peace—not only in the Ukraine, but worldwide—is the Norwegian NGO, Nobel Peace Prize Watch,[112] in Oslo, which has launched a *Nordic Initiative for Peace in Ukraine and Lasting World Peace.* This organization is headed by a Norwegian lawyer, Fredrik Heffermehl, who has published an important book[113] on the last will and testament of Alfred Nobel and on the necessity to stop the politicization of the NPP and ensure that it is only conferred to persons who have significantly advanced the peace goals as formulated by Alfred Nobel in his last will and testament. This thorough legal analysis of the NPP demonstrates that 120 years after its establishment, the realization of the specific peace ideal of Afred Nobel has become an existential necessity for the survival of humanity. In a world of nuclear weapons, it is imperative to have a preventive strategy and multiple contingency plans to ensure that the world does not stumble into a nuclear confrontation. While the NPP could contribute to peace-making by supporting every effort at mediation and compromise, and

112 *The Nobel Peace Prize Watch,* http://nobelwill.org/.
113 Fredrik S. Heffermehl, *The Nobel Peace Prize: What Nobel Really Wanted* (Westport, Conn.: Praeger, 2010), http://nobelwill.org/index.html?tab=3; http://www. nobelwill.org/bookorder2.html.

honoring persons genuinely committed to peace, the prize has been transformed into a political weapon and has been repeatedly awarded to warmongers and war criminals.

On April 28, 2022 the Nobel Peace Prize Watch sent the letter below to the five heads of state of the Nordic countries proposing a Nordic Initiative for peace.[114] I was among the nine scholars who were invited to co-sign the initiative.

A Nordic Initiative for Peace in Ukraine and Lasting World Peace

2 May 2022

Fredrik S. Heffermehl | Nobel Peace Prize Watch— TRANSCEND Media Service

To: *The Honorable Prime Ministers of the five Nordic countries: Magdalena Anderson, Mette Frederiksen, Katrín Jakobsdóttir, Sanna Marin, and Jonas Gahr Støre*

Oslo, 27 April, 2022—The war in Ukraine once again shows that the world is like a city with brutal gangs constantly roaming the streets, looting and fighting with loads of heavy weapons. No one will ever feel safe in such a city. The same applies at the international level. No amount of weaponry can make us safe. No country will be safe until also neighboring countries can feel safe. The present international system is broken; to avoid future wars we need deep reforms.

Once again, now in Ukraine, we have seen that arms cannot prevent war. We should not, in the present state of shock, expand or prolong the militarist traditions that guarantee eternal war and, in the nuclear age, a constant risk of annihilation. Our recommendation is that the five Nordic countries together take an initiative to activate the UN goals of global democracy and collective security. In a renewed UN, the

---

114 Nobel Peace Prize Watch, "A Nordic Initiative for Peace in Ukraine and Lasting World Peace," *Free Press,* April 28, 2022, https://freepress.org/article/nordic-initiative-peace-ukraine-and-lasting-world-peace.

member nations should act in loyal co-operation and take their charter obligations seriously. A most promising step here was yesterday's resolution in the General Assembly curbing the Security Council veto.

A way out of stalled negotiations can be a major shift of perspective or arena. Mindful that Mikhail Gorbachev called for a disarmament race, and Vladimir Putin has repeatedly proposed a law-based international order, it seems to us that an end to the Ukraine war might be reached by making it part of ending the wider, geopolitical war between the U.S. and Russia.

Fear of U.S. expansion does, of course, not justify Russia's attack on Ukraine. And yet, it is troubling that the U.S., with a 40% share of the world's military budgets and 97% of the military bases abroad, seems to be seeking more influence. The Nordic countries should carefully consider whether four U.S. bases (Norway), NATO membership (Finland, Sweden), further arms purchases (all), will improve their security. Only a year ago the outgoing U.S. president released an attack on Congress. The U.S. power of coercive diplomacy is waning. It is imperative to take the time necessary to thoroughly evaluate the developing world situation and the legitimacy and dangers of taking irreversible steps to increase U.S. power.

Facing a stream of global crises, humanity can no longer afford wars. We need to cooperate, build solidarity and trust with effective, common enforcement of international law. Instead of complicity in future war crimes, how much more tempting must it not be to instead engineer a Nordic initiative to realize the collective security provisions of the UN Charter?

The Nordic countries enjoy trust and credibility in the world. They are particularly well positioned for an initiative to empower the Security Council and enable it to fulfill its responsibility for maintaining peace. This will require nations to transfer a part of their sovereignty, which Norway and Denmark already have prepared for.* Instead of more NATO, the world urgently needs to unite across all borders, ethnic and religious divisions, political and economic systems, to rebuild, empower and recommit to the United Nations, build peace, and reallocate the expenditures for war to serve the needs of people and nature.

With reverent greetings,

NOBEL PEACE PRIZE WATCH
Fredrik S. Heffermehl, Oslo

* * *

We agree in the essence and would welcome a Nordic peace initiative:

Richard Falk, Santa Barbara
Bruce Kent, London
Tomas Magnusson, Gothenburg
Mairead Maguire, Belfast
David Swanson, Virginia
Alfred de Zayas, Geneva
Jan Öberg, Lund
Hans Christof von Sponeck,
Klaus Schlichtmann, Tokyo

THE FUNCTIONS
OF LAW

23.

The Rule of Law Must Finally Evolve Into the Rule of Justice

Many politicians, academics, and media pundits are wont to invoke the "rule of law," a "rules-based international order," "values diplomacy," etc. But what do all these benevolent-sounding slogans actually mean in practice? Who makes the rules, who interprets them, who enforces them? What transparency and accountability accompany these noble pledges?

In a very real sense, we already have a "rules based international order" in the form of the UN Charter and its "supremacy clause," article 103 of which grants it priority over all other treaties and agreements. The norms established in the Charter are rational, but effective enforcement mechanisms are yet to be created.

We also have humanistic "values" that should guide diplomacy and peace-making—including the principle *"pacta sunt servanda"* (treaties must be implemented, art. 26 of the Vienna Convention on the law of treaties). Let us not forget the general principles of law, including good faith (*bona fide*), the prohibition of abusing rights (*sic utere tuo ut alienum non laedas*), and the principle of estoppel (*ex injuria non oritur jus*)—you can't have your cake and eat it.

Alas, both in domestic and international law there is a high level of bad faith and the tendency to apply double standards. Major powers make agreements and then break them with impunity. They undermine diplomacy by brazenly lying, by making promises and not keeping them. This subverts the credibility of the entire system of norms and mechanisms which has been so arduously established and agreed to. Politicians often forget that keeping one's word is not only a matter of personal honor—it is an indispensable element of trust in the conduct of public affairs. Among other crucial values that we should promote are Christian values such as compassion, empathy, forgiveness, solidarity.

It is axiomatic that the rule of law functions as a pillar of stability, predictability and the democratic ethos in modern society. Its object and purpose is to serve the human person and progressively achieve human dignity in the larger context of freedom.

Because law reflects power imbalances, we must ensure that the ideal of the rule of law is not instrumentalized simply to enforce the status quo, maintain privilege, and the exploitation of one group over another. The rule of law must be a rule that allows flexibility and welcomes continuous democratic dialogue to devise and implement those reforms required by an evolving society. It must be a rule of conscience, of listening.

Throughout history law has all too frequently been manipulated by political power, becoming a kind of dictatorship through law, where people are robbed of their individual and collective rights, while the law itself becomes the main instrument of their disenfranchisement. Experience has taught us that law is not coterminous with justice and that laws can be adopted and enforced to perpetuate abuse and cement injustice. Accordingly, any appeal to the rule of law should be contextualized within a human-rights-based framework.

Already in Sophocles' drama *Antigone* we saw the clash between the arbitrary law of King Creon and the unwritten law of humanity. Enforcing Creon's unjust law brought misery to all. In Roman times the maxim *dura lex sed lex* (the law is hard, but it is the law) was mellowed by Cicero's wise reminder that *summum jus summa injuria* (extreme law is extreme injustice, *de Officiis* 1, 10, 33), i.e. the blind application of the law may cause great injustice.

The contention that, irrespective of what it stipulates, "the law must be obeyed" has been challenged by human rights heroes for thousands of years.

- Spartacus fought against the Roman slave laws and paid with his life. Slavery remained constitutional and legal in the Western hemisphere until the mid-nineteenth century.

- Colonialism was deemed constitutional and legal by the colonizers until the decolonization processes of the 1950s, 1960s and 1970s.

- Nazi Germany's racist Nuremberg laws of 1935 were constitutional and legal in that state, as were those of South Africa's Apartheid;

- Stalin's laws, the Holodomor in the Ukraine and the purges of the 1930s were all based on Soviet laws and decrees.

- Segregation in the U.S. was constitutional and legal (see, for instance, the U.S. Supreme Court judgment *Plessy v. Ferguson*) until overturned in 1954.

Civil disobedience, inter alia by Henry David Thoreau, Zaghioul Pasha, Michael Collins, Dietrich Bonhoeffer, Mahatma Gandhi, Martin Luther King, Nelson Mandela, Ken Saro Wiwa, Mohamed Bouazizi, was legitimate and necessary to give example and initiate reforms—but they all suffered the consequences of having opposed the fetishism of the "rule of law."

Human justice in the twenty-first century requires that the rule of law as expressed in the international world order cease being the rule of power, of might makes right, geopolitics and economics. The rule of law must incorporate human dignity into the equation and enable people power, self-determination and referenda. The international rule of law must evolve into the rule of social justice and peace.

Indeed, a civilization does not simply require society to have a set of laws and a powerful police force to enforce them. Civilization means ensuring the real welfare of people, creating the conditions necessary for their pursuit of happiness. The true indicators of civilization are not an expanding Gross Domestic Product, ever-growing consumption, and aggressive exploitation of natural resources—but rather respect for human and animal life; sustainable management of the environment; local, regional and international solidarity; social justice and a culture of peace.

Unfortunately, Western civilization does not measure up with its noble ideals. Our governments continue to sabotage the rule of law by instrumentalizing norms to destroy justice, e.g. by weaponizing extradition law to persecute whistle-blowers like Julian Assange to keep them bottled up for decades.

Similarly, the extradition of Alex Saab from Cape Verde in 2021 to a kangaroo trial in the United States is a travesty of justice, as was the prosecution and imprisonment of the "Cuban 5," victims of gross political injustice by a Miami tribunal. We have witnessed the increased use of "lawfare" to destroy political adversaries, e.g. the frame-up of Dilma Rousseff in Brazil, making the way free for "regime change." Or take the subversion of election monitoring by the Organization of American States resulting in the *coup d'état* against Evo Morales of Bolivia in 2019. And then there's the lawfare in Ecuador exercised against former President Rafael Correa and former Vice-President Jorge Glas (recently released after years of arbitrary arrest and persecution).[115]

Considerable responsibility for the corruption of the rule of law is borne by the corporate media that systematically disinforms the public about the facts and imposes a "managed narrative" that essentially cripples any chance for an objective debate. Over the past decades the corporate media has engaged in brazen propaganda to create a false "perception" of the law, including international law, that is very distant from any conception of justice. By suppressing information, disinforming and whitewashing, the corporate media has become complicit in the war crimes and crimes against humanity perpetrated in Afghanistan, Iraq, Syria, Libya, Yemen, etc. The media has even

---

115 Ronald Ángel, "Ecuador: The key elements to the release of Jorge Glas and what could happen with Lasso's appeal," elciudadano.com,, April 12, 2022, https://www.elciudadano.com/en/ecuador-the-key-elements-to-the-release-of-jorge-glas-and-what-could-happen-with-lassos-appeal/04/12/

attempted to create the impression that the 2003 Invasion of Iraq, which then UN Secretary General Kofi Annan has repeatedly called an "illegal war," was actually a "just war" in keeping with the UN Charter.

Bottom line: in order to help the rule of law evolve into the rule of justice, we must demand our right to access to information. We must adopt a Charter of Rights of Whistle-blowers, demand transparency and accountability from our governments, and ensure that Parliaments revisit obsolete laws that perpetuate injustice. We must remain vigilant to ensure that the rule of justice is built and maintained day by day and that our courts and tribunals apply the existing legislation in good faith and not in the service of corporations and special interests, who do not want rights—but only privileges.

24.

Reflections on Law and Justice

The old adage that Justice is blind is being challenged by many lawyers and sociologists who maintain that Justice cannot be neutral, that the function of justice is to condemn the bad and protect the good. Hence the question arises whether Justice is neutral or teleological? This frequently asked question is ultimately artificial. The tension between the two options can be resolved.

Justice, like truth, is an absolute term. But an absolute term with nuances!

What we mean is that the *process* to arrive at justice must be objective and impartial, so as to facilitate a just and equitable result. Moreover, we must not amalgamate the concepts of "law" and "Justice," which admittedly overlap. In fact, they frequently mean different things and can even be opposites. While Justice is a form of ethics, a metaphysical value related to truth, law is a man-made norm or "rule of the game" that always remains work-in-progress, by nature incomplete and time-bound, thus frequently opportunistic, obsolete, lagging behind the times.

The vocation of the administration of Justice is to practice "fairness" and impartiality so as to strengthen what is good, redress wrongs and protect the oppressed. In this sense, Justice (the outcome) cannot be neutral, and by necessity must be teleological. What must be neutral is the methodology to arrive at and to enforce Justice even-handedly, uniformly, predictably.

A judge must start every judicial investigation with an open mind, proactively seek all relevant facts, double-check sources, consider all the information obtainable, listen to all arguments— *audiatur et altera pars*—look for motivation, weigh-in merit, performance, put events into context, so as to be better able formulate a reasoned opinion. But this conclusion, a judgment arrived at through objective methodology, can no longer be "neutral"—otherwise the whole fact-finding and evaluation procedure would be useless.

A judge does justice by establishing the facts and applying law non-selectively, rejecting double-standards. Yet, neutrality does not mean blindness, and the judge should never become a computer who automatically and perfunctorily applies the laws without considering the specific circumstances and the probable consequences, because statutes and norms themselves may be deliberately or inadvertently unjust—such as much of tax legislation with its built-in loopholes for the rich, legislation establishing privileges and tax havens, legal constructs that facilitate money-laundering, the old laws on slavery and the slave trade, Apartheid laws, *Kafala* norms, Hitler's Nuremberg laws, land-grabbing laws, etc.

The judge must keep the spirit of the law in mind and try to interpret legislation—and a country's Constitution—accordingly. Beyond applying the statutes in force, the judge must respect the underlying "general principles of law" (article 38 of the ICJ statute). Among these general principles are good faith, the necessity to listen to all sides (*audiatur et altera pars*), reciprocity, estoppel, the "clean hands" doctrine, the "do no harm" rule (going back to Greek and Roman law, *primum nil nocere*), the rule against abuse of rights *(sic utere tuo ut alienum non laedas*), the rule that no one can derive benefit from his own violations of law (*ex injuria non oritur jus),* and the relevance of cause and effect.

If Justice were mathematics, one would not need judges, but only computers. That is why an appeal to "natural law" is frequently made, precisely because many statutes actually perpetuate injustice. As Cicero put it, "*summum jus, summa injuria*"—an excess of law, or the blind application of the law can lead to gravest injustice. Themis, the Greek goddess of Justice, was not blindfolded; she carried a sword to separate fact from fiction, and to make clear that her decisions were fast and final. When Themis was ignored, Nemesis, the goddess of revenge, would impose retribution.

Since the 16th century, *Iustitia*, the Roman goddess of Justice, sometimes called Lady Justice, is often depicted wearing a blindfold, a metaphor suggesting impartiality, since Justice must decide without preferences according to race, color, religion, political opinion, or social status. The blindfold, however, was an unwise innovation that has done more harm than good. Indeed, a judge must not be blind, but instead sharpen his vision so as to recognize the occurrence of the abuse of power through law, what today is sometimes referred to as "lawfare": the instrumentalization of law as a weapon to destabilize and destroy economic or political adversaries. While responsible for ensuring that "justice is done," a judge must do this with open eyes and ears, interpreting and applying statutes and jurisprudence in context and with flexibility, understanding and vision, so that fairness and equity prevail.

In order to arrive at Justice, law must create a framework that is both preventive and curative; it should nourish an environment where Justice can flourish, where the administration of justice is impartial and has credibility by virtue of its clarity and predictability. Justice cannot be achieved through a "*tabula rasa*" approach, disregarding the prevalence of historical inequities, existing imbalances and privileges. The continuation of these inequities is incompatible with Justice, which is not mere rhetoric or proforma compliance with law but requires a continuous implementation of rights and obligations and a conscious redressing of wrongs so that all human beings can pursue their well-being in larger freedom—and in solidarity with the rest of society.

Whereas Justice is the goal, law is only one of the many ways to advance toward Justice. Other avenues are truth and reparation commissions, emergency decrees, social activism, humanistic and religious *caritas*. Yet, in many countries, including those with democratic governments, law can be used to impede Justice, undermine and frustrate it. Justice must be contextual and universal. By its very nature, all legal regimes are incomplete, because the legislature does not enact all the laws that may be necessary, nor does it abrogate all the laws that have become obsolete. Law is punctual, aimed at addressing a particular issue, and rarely can it incorporate all relevant facets and factors. Thus, in most cases, law cannot and should not be considered as absolute, sacred, categorical or inexorable—but instead must allow for flexibility in its interpretation and application. It is the function of judges to interpret the law in a manner that will advance Justice.

The law may be blind—but the judges must never be. Nor can the judges capitulate to positivism by allowing the letter of the law to corrupt and deny the spirit of the law.

25.

Reflections on Law and Punishment

Law and punishment are very different concepts and should not be unduly amalgamated. The function of law is the codification of norms, definition of rights and obligations, and the creation of mechanisms for monitoring and enforcement. Law must be both preventive and curative. It should be proactive and not merely reactive.

Punishment is always *ex post facto* and is therefore an unsatisfactory "Plan B," after Plan A has failed. It is far more important for law to lay down safeguards so as to avert the breach of law and irreparable harm. It is perhaps bizarre that recently many human rights activists, non-governmental organizations and the bulk of the media have embraced punishment as a kind of preferred Kalashnikov. The *Zeitgeist* has embraced an over-simplification: punishment as *the* principal legal tool, as a weapon of fear and deterrence. In their binary world of good and evil, it's rightful that evil be suppressed through "lawfare" and, as seems more apparent than ever, through the instrumentalization of the International Criminal Court to target some, but not all criminals.

The letter and spirit of the law requires, however, that law be much more than meting out penalties and sanctions against those who do not observe the established administrative, civil and criminal regimes, which are man-made and, in many situations, constitute very imperfect or even deliberately unjust regimes that perpetuate imbalances and protect privilege. Natural law and common sense require that codified law be modified so as to take the evolution of society into account and ensure that Justice prevails.

There is a peculiar *fetishism* about the concept of punishment as an essential part of Justice. However, this simplistic concept has always been flawed, because multiple factors other than *culpa* lead to a breach of the law. The "*lex talionis*" (an eye for an eye) has no place in enlightened societies. Indeed, punishment can be considered a legitimate tool only if it has a *deterrent* effect, and if it educates society how to better live together. There is deterrence when one knows that illegally parking and exceeding the speed limits are risky activities, and if the perpetrator is caught, then traffic tickets or fines eloquently drive the point home. Yet, when punishment becomes mere revenge, the result may well be counter-productive and engender greater injustice and instability. What is important is to break the vicious circle of violence and repression.

Experience shows that punishment has all too often been applied selectively and has been used as a weapon of domination. Neither law nor Justice are mathematical sciences. Both are anthropocentric and must serve humanity by facilitating moral and material rehabilitation of the criminal and reconciliation with society.

Seeing the perpetrators of a breach of law punished does not undo the offense, does not necessarily advance the goal of preventing future offenses, does not make victims whole, nor does it strengthen a peaceful society based on law, mutual respect, and ethical values. What is important is to give recognition, respect, and reparation to victims of injustice, violence, and breaches of human dignity. One way to achieve redress is to establish truth and reconciliation commissions. Another avenue may be provided by peoples' tribunals.

Moreover, the law must not discriminate among victims. The concept of a hierarchy of victims, the "sorting out" of victims, the competition among victims are all unworthy of a legal order aimed at achieving Justice. When the law creates categories of victims that are "politically correct" and tolerates that other victims are ignored, it corrupts the concept of Justice, because all victims deserve our attention and compassion. All victims are equal in their human dignity and deserve recognition and reparation, without discrimination.

Just as law and Justice are not coterminous, the concept of law should be decoupled from that of punishment. But whenever punishment is imposed, the courts must demonstrate that such punishment will be met uniformly to all who have broken the law.

In this context, it is worth recalling that, at the opening of the Nuremberg Trials in October 1945, United States chief prosecutor Robert Jackson stated:

> We must never forget that the record on which we judge these defendants today is the record on which history will judge us tomorrow .... While this law is first applied against German aggressors, the law includes, and if it is to serve a useful purpose it must condemn, aggression by any other nations, including those which sit here now in judgment."[116]

In this sense the 1946 Judgment of the Tribunal stipulated that "To initiate a war of aggression ... is ... the supreme international crime differing only from other war crimes in that it contains within itself the accumulated evil of the whole."[117]

Unfortunately for all humanity, the noble words of Robert Jackson and the Judgment of the Tribunal did not result in deterrence of aggressive war, did not educate the world in the ways of peace, as those same countries who sat in judgment over the Nazi war criminals themselves continued pursuing their geo-political and geo-economic agendas, continued to start wars of aggression and commit egregious war crimes. The lessons of Nuremberg were not learned.

---

116 *Trial of the Major War Criminals Before the International Military Tribunal, Nuremberg, 14 November 1945 - 1 October 1946,* Vol. 2, 101.

117 Ibid., Vol. 22, p. 427.

PAX ET JUSTITIA

The motto of the International Labour Organization, *si vis pacem cole justitiam*—if you want peace, cultivate Justice— expresses a fundamental truth that many politicians have pondered but somehow failed to implement. Indeed, if there is no social justice, if laws do not fulfil their preventive and cura- tive functions, domestic and international conflicts inevitably result. That is why law is crucial in providing a solid framework and educating society about those fundamental human rights and freedoms that will gradually advance humanity toward Justice and Peace. We need education for peace and empathy, education in the spirit of the UN Charter and the UNESCO Constitution. *Pax et Justitia* must become the tangible cultural heritage of humankind.

26.

No Right Arises from a Wrong

"Getting away with it" does not render blatant aggression any less criminal. Aggression remains a supreme crime, as Chief Prosecutor Robert Jackson said in his opening statement at the Nuremberg Trials in 1945. Getting away with such a crime does not and cannot legalize it, it only manifests the inadequacy of the administration of international criminal justice and of the political institutions responsible for the enforcement of the "rule of law."

- The U.S. aggressions against Vietnam, Laos and Cambodia 1963–75;

- the NATO countries' aggression against Yugoslavia in 1999 and against Afghanistan in the 20-year war 2001–2021;

- the assault on Iraq by the "coalition of the willing" in 2003;

- the military interventions in Libya and Syria since 2011;

- Saudi Arabia's ongoing genocidal war against Yemen;

- Azerbaijan's *Blitzkrieg* against the hapless Armenians of Nagorno Karabakh;

- Russia's "special military operation"/war against Ukraine since February 2022:

All of these armed conflicts entailed the crime of aggression and engendered egregious war crimes that hitherto have remained unpunished.

An objective investigation of all the crimes committed after the entry into force of the Statute of Rome should be conducted by the International Criminal Court. Those responsible for giving the orders and for implementing them should be prosecuted. Aggressive war is not only illegal—it is madness, the *ultima irratio.*

The prevailing impunity of the powerful does not legalize their crimes. However, "precedents of impunity" since 1945 have weakened the fabric of international law and undermined the authority and credibility of the United Nations as a peace-making and peace-ensuring organization. Again and again, the United Nations has failed to silence the drums of war and stop impending aggressions. It famously failed to stop the brazen assault on Iraq on March 20, 2003 in which the 43 countries of the "coalition of the willing" rebelled against the UN Charter. It actually facilitated the aggression against Libya in 2011 through the adoption of SC resolution 1973. In 2005 the General Assembly had invented the concept of "responsibility to protect," initially sold and marketed to the world as a proactive mechanism to protect hostage civilian populations when their governments failed to protect them. But in actuality, R2P proved to be a particularly perverse scam, as we recognize from its abuse in Libya and elsewhere, a harmless sounding scheme concocted to accommodate the attempt by some powerful governments to circumvent the prohibition of the use of force contained in article 2 (4) of the UN Charter.

While article 2(4) prohibits both the use of force and the *threat of the use of force*, the UN Security Council and General Assembly have failed to take any concrete action to condemn warmongering and sabre-rattling. Although article 20 of the International Covenant on Civil and Political Rights specifically prohibits propaganda for war and incitement to racial hatred and violence, the Human Rights Committee has never done much to identify the multiple violators, primarily the powerful States that have hijacked human rights and weaponized them against geopolitical rivals for purposes of making enforced regime change appear somehow legitimate.

It is important to emphasize that, notwithstanding the media fanfare about R2P, the hypocritical practice of invoking "humanitarian intervention" as a pretext to topple foreign governments has not generated and cannot generate any valid legal precedent because, as the general principle of law—*ex injuria non oritur jus*—dictates, a right cannot arise from a wrong. Breaking international law cannot engender a new "customary international law." Accordingly, military incursions without approval of the UN Security Council are neither legal nor "legitimate." Yet, we observe how bogus arguments are wielded to construct a perception of "legitimacy." These are intellectually dishonest games—games that cost tens of thousands of human lives.

Of course, the rule of law and international order have been wounded again and again—but they are not yet dead. Punishment still awaits the offenders whenever the International Criminal Court is prepared to take the Rome Statute seriously and to prosecute the larger-than-life criminals and not just vanquished enemies or ousted politicians. Neither "exceptionalism" nor "legal black holes" are compatible with the international human rights treaty regime. Aggression remains the ultimate crime because it leads to war crimes and crimes against humanity. Yet, the merchants of death in the military-industrial-financial complex love their wars and their profits.

PERCEPTIONS OF LEGITIMACY

When it is impossible to justify some action in terms of legality, politicians sometimes turn to the more ambiguous, less juridical term: "legitimacy." For example, during the Yugoslav and Iraq wars many "legal experts" and some compromised professors of international law contended that while those military operations were not *strictu sensu* legal, because they had not been approved by the United Nations, they were "legitimate," and in this context they invoked the obsolete concept of a "just war," which essentially was disavowed with the adoption of the UN Charter. In the post-1945 international order, no use of force is legal unless approved by the Security Council, and by virtue of the "supremacy clause" (article 103 of the UN Charter) the

Charter prohibition trumps all other treaties and arrangements. Notwithstanding international law doctrine, there are many State practices that systematically violate the UN Charter, human rights conventions and customary international law. Hitherto there is no palpable consequences for the violators.

Another illegal practice is the imposition of unilateral coercive measures, which has been condemned numerous times by the United Nations General Assembly, most recently in resolution 76/161 of December 2021 and by the Human Rights Council in its resolution 46/5 of March 2021. The U.S. embargo against Cuba has been condemned in 29 separate resolutions by the General Assembly, most recently in resolution 75/289 in June 2021, and yet the embargo and sanctions persist. The damage caused to the Cuban economy over the past sixty years is phenomenal, but no one in the western mainstream media cares to inform readers about the UN Secretary General's annual reports documenting the adverse human rights impacts of the sanctions and financial blockade.

It is true that only a handful of States impose such sanctions, but these are the very powerful and rich states, and thus far they have gotten away with it. Has this created a new norm in international law? Has this modified customary international law in any way? No. *Ex injuria non oritur jus.* As evidenced by the voting record of the vast majority of States members of the United Nations in the General Assembly and Human Rights Council, such measures are deemed to be contrary to the UN Charter. All that this shows is that the UN lacks an effective mechanism for the enforcement of international law and its prohibitions.

Of course, we live in a world of fake news and fake law, supported by certain governments and the media. As various UN reports document, economic sanctions cause the death of tens of thousands of children and adults from malnutrition, lack of medicines, lack of medical equipment. This justifies classifying such sanctions in the category of crimes against humanity for purposes of article 7 of the Statute of Rome, even if the

International Criminal Court, which thus far has been in the service of the powerful, has not indicted any person in connection with illegal unilateral coercive measures.

An additional problem is the on-going corruption of language and concepts through the "information war" conducted by intelligence services and echoed by the corporate media, which seldom reports on unilateral coercive measures, and when they do they try to convey the impression that sanctions are morally justified and legal. Seldom do you read in the pages of *The New York Times* or *Washington Post* that these sanctions contravene a host of international norms, including the principle of State sovereignty, the self-determination of peoples, the prohibition in interfering in the internal affairs of states, the principle of freedom of commerce and freedom of navigation. Therefore, the public at large tends to concede sanctions a presumption of legitimacy.

As shown above, thanks to the steady brainwashing through the corporate media, the imperial practice of imposing "unilateral coercive measures" and the idea of "humanitarian intervention" have attained a measure of acceptance, although they violate the UN Charter and general principles of law. When we look at the so-called humanitarian interventions in Yugoslavia, Iraq, Libya and Syria, where tens of thousands of human beings were killed, we realize that these were classical geopolitical crimes, even if they were sold to the public by means of the jargon of human rights. Their purposes were strictly geopolitical and economic, aiming at undemocratic "regime change."

Even more perverse than the human and material damage visited on the targeted countries, is the resulting weakening of the authority and credibility of international law and of the international institutions charged with monitoring and enforcing it. These "humanitarian interventions"/wars have engendered serious global repercussions owing to the way Western powers have attempted to give the impression that a valid international legal precedent was being set. Needless to say, government lawyers in the West, together with those in Turkey and Saudi Arabia, understood full well that the violation of Syria's sovereignty with warplanes and cruise missiles entailed gross violations of international law, but the lawyers knew how to camouflage these aggressions as "reprisals" for non-existent chemical attacks and other false flag operations.

Here we are confronted not only with "fake news" used to justify acts of aggression, but with "fake law," pretending that violating international law would actually change international law.

A number of Western authors and journalists claimed that, by going ahead and striking Syrian territory illegally, customary international law itself was being changed. In the West the attacks on Syrian government targets in 2015–21 were often described as "Grotian moments"[118]—events which marked "a fundamental change in the existing international system," which some Western pundits claimed sparked a major reformation of customary international law pertaining to crimes of aggression. This argument was based on the premise that, since the Western powers had used alleged humanitarian abuses in the form of chemical attacks as pretexts to strike Syria, attacking other countries on similar grounds should henceforth be considered legal. The countries intervening in Syria without approval of the Security Council were consciously violating international law, but they knew that although their actions fell within the Kampala definition of aggression, adopted by the Assembly of State parties to the Rome Statute in 2010, the likelihood that the International Criminal Court would ever take up the matter was minimal.

As A.B. Abrams writes in his book *World War in Syria*,[119] although the radical premise that the West could so fundamentally alter international law unilaterally was and is entirely contrary

---

118 Hugo Grotius (1583–1645), Dutch scholar considered the "father of international law."

119 A.B. Abrams, *World War in Syria* (Atlanta, Ga.: Clarity Press, 2021).

to international law itself, this still finds considerable support across the Western media. The idea that when the Western powers commit a crime, that action somehow evolves into an international norm and therefore a new part of customary law, reminds me of a 1972 statement by U.S. President Nixon who claimed following the Watergate scandal : "Well, when the president does it that means that it is not illegal."[120] In this context "the president" could be replaced by the West and the subjects by the rest of the world. Thus, the narrative was advanced that if Western actions were illegal, it could only be because customary international law was obsolete and needed to be reformed to make them the "new normal." The West itself, like "the president," could not be in the wrong—an argument which reflects an ideology of not just of U.S. but of Western exceptionalism.

Bottom line: There is no way that the world at large will accept the proposition that the Europeans and Americans are the ones who set the rules, and that the West now has every legal right to attack them if it could claim a moral pretext to do so. This has a highly destabilising impact on the global order, and we see the effects of the corruption of the perception of law in the mainstream narrative concerning the war in Ukraine. Certainly, the Chinese, the Russians, the Indians, the Pakistanis, the Indonesians, the South Africans, the Venezuelans etc. will reject Western hubris and insist on full participation in the drafting and adoption of any new international law rules. As it stands, the only "world constitution" is the United Nations Charter, which lays out a "rules based international order," if only the States would care to implement it.

---

120 Helen Dewar, "President Isn't Above the Law, Nixon Insists," *Washington Post,* June 5, 1977.

27.

Who Will Ensure that the Guardians of the Rule of Law Do Not Themselves Betray It?

As we surf the mainstream media, listen to the *telejournal,* and check out social media, we can witness how fake news evolves into fake history and how politicians and journalists instrumentalize both to concoct fake law. I think that we can say, without fear of contradiction, that there is a veritable war on truth. Surely, we are on a slippery slope toward fake democracy—or are we already there?

Quis custodiet ipsos custodes? (Juvenalis, *Satires*)— Who will stand watch over the guardians?—when the mainstream media no longer performs the function of the watchdog, no longer alerts us to endemic—and immediate— governmental abuses but act more like echo-chambers of the interests of certain "elites" and transnational corporations. . . . Who will blow the whistle on governmental and private-sector scams? How can we defend our rights when our elected officials, those who have the obligation to uphold the law, are actually in the service of other, more powerful and lucrative interests? What can we do when the executive, legislative and judiciary are progressively corrupted, when institutions like the ICC discontinue investigations into gross criminality by powerful states while prosecuting the little fish, when the Organization for the Prohibition of Chemical Weapons tampers with the evidence of its own inspectors and suppresses crucial facts (per the Douma "report" on Syria), when the OAS is complicit in a coup d'état against an OAS member state (Bolivia), when other supposedly objective organizations systematically disinform the public, disseminate evidence-free news, and suppress dissent?

Only we can be the guardians—by reclaiming democracy and our right to effective participation in public affairs, as stipulated in article 25 of the International Covenant on Civil and Political Rights. We must condemn the politicization and "weaponization" of human rights, especially when human entitlements of some are instrumentalized to obliterate others.

We should remember that human rights are not in competition with each other, but that human rights constitute a holistic system based on our common human dignity. We know that the United Nations, the Security Council, the General Assembly, ECOSOC, the Human Rights Council are all political institutions. That's not the problem—it is a *factum* that everything can be seen as "political" in some way. What is crucial is that everybody be required to play by the same rules and that there be some kind of monitoring to ensure that the rules are being observed in good faith.

One problem lies in the fact that many diplomats and politicians sitting in public institutions do not really feel committed to human rights, international law or international solidarity—or at least do not consider these values as their priorities, although they give the requisite lip service to them. Another problem lies in the absence of ethics in public institutions, in the double standards used by politicians and diplomats.

Surely, the world needs a rules-based international order—valid for everybody, not just as applied against the poorer countries. Remarkably, the U.S. Secretary of State Antony Blinken keeps harping on the need for a "rules based" order even while ignoring the rules of the one we already have: the United Nations Charter, which is akin to a world constitution. The necessary framework is already provided by the Charter. All we have to do it is to apply it in good faith.

It is dismaying to see how many countries ostensibly committed to the International Covenant on Civil and Political

Rights and the International Covenant on Economic, Social and Cultural Rights, systematically vote in the Human Rights Council to defeat certain mandates that advance transparency and accountability, voting against the human right to peace, the right to international solidarity, the right to development. How can we denounce countries that sabotage efforts to adopt a legally binding instrument on corporate social responsibility, flout the prohibition on unilateral coercive measures, use mercenaries to defeat the right of self-determination of peoples, and disregard UN decisions and resolutions, including Advisory Opinions of the International Court of Justice?

Powerful States that routinely violate international law with impunity are actually sending a dangerous signal to developing countries in Africa, Asia and Latin America that there actually is no international order but rather chaos and the right of the strongest. If we in the developed "West" want to be leaders—not only in economic matters, but also in human rights, we must lead by good example. And when we do evil things like the barbaric assault on Iraq in 2003 or the persecution of "whistle-blowers" like Julian Assange and Edward Snowden, we establish "precedents of permissibility" if not of law—which others will surely follow. Therein lies the curse of evil deeds—that they continue generating other evils—*"Das eben ist der Fluch der bösen Tat, dass sie fortzeugend Böses muss gebären"* (Friedrich von Schiller, *Piccolomini*).

What the international community needs in the twenty-first century is mutual respect, multipolarity and international solidarity. And yet, from all sides we experience the pressures of Orwellian narratives, conformism and "political correctness." We must be very vigilant if we do not want to get caught up in a totalitarian witch hunt against "wrongthink."

We ourselves must be both guardians and whistle-blowers. We cannot trust institutions that are financed by corporations and/or have been penetrated by intelligence services. We cannot rely on media that only acts as echo chambers of the powerful.

We must pro-actively build a sustainable world—day by day—based on the United Nations Charter and multilateral action. *We are the guardians.*

THE FUTURE OF
HUMAN RIGHTS

28.

Peng Chun Chang and the Holistic Approach to Human Rights

Seventy-three years ago, in the early hours of December 10, 1948, the UN General Assembly was meeting at the Palais Chaillot in Paris. The previous night the Assembly had just adopted the Convention on the Prevention and Punishment of the Crime of Genocide, and the meeting continued past midnight to adopt the Universal Declaration of Human Rights, an essential addendum to the UN Charter. This remarkable document which has been translated into 500 languages, reflects a universal commitment to human dignity and constitutes a Magna Carta for all humankind.

The principal drafters of the declaration were the American President of the UN Commission on Human Rights, Eleanor Roosevelt, the French legal expert René Cassin, the Lebanese diplomat Charles Malik and the Chinese philosopher and diplomat P.C. Chang (1892–1957). The document was a collaborative effort by representatives of all regions of the world, assisted by the logistical and substantive support of the UN Secretariat under the Canadian law professor, John Humphrey.

It is extraordinary that the notable intellectual contribution of Malik and Chang has been largely overlooked by historians and the media, at least thus far, but recently a book was published by Swedish Professor Hans Ingvar Roth, *P.C. Chang and the Universal Declaration*, which is likely to change that perception. Indeed, it was Chang who, more than anyone else, infused philosophy into the document, in particular the global and cross-cultural perspective. Without a doubt, Chang deserves credit for the universality and religious ecumenism of the declaration, for its holistic approach to civil, cultural, economic, political, and social rights.

Born in Tianjin, Chang led a multifaceted life. He taught philosophy at Nankai University in Tianjin and became a renowned scholar of Chinese traditional drama and Peking opera. In the 1930s he led the Chinese Classical Theatre on tour to North America and the Soviet Union, but following Japan's invasion of China in 1937, Chang joined the resistance and eventually had to flee the country. He was crucial in promoting awareness in Europe and America of the Nanking genocide, where as many as 300,000 Chinese were massacred by the Japanese.

In 1942 Chang became a full-time diplomat and served as China's ambassador to Turkey, where he enthusiastically disseminated knowledge about Chinese history and culture, its silks and porcelains, its literature and philosophy. An expert on the political thought of Confucius (551–479 BC), he also promoted knowledge about the ethics of Meng-tse (Mencius, 372–289 BC) and stressed that diplomacy should advance virtue, its noblest goal being to "subdue people with goodness." He enlightened many about the influence of Chinese philosophy on European thinkers, including Voltaire and Diderot.

As Vice-President of the UN Commission on Human Rights, Chang inspired delegations by his Renaissance knowledge and modesty. He promoted ancient and up-to-date ideas of Chinese philosophers—not because they were Chinese, but because they were universally valid.

In the course of the 1950s, the holistic approach to human rights was abandoned by the Commission on Human Rights and the Universal Declaration was split into two categories of rights: on the one side the individualistic "business friendly" rights, on the other the social, economic and cultural rights, requiring governmental investment in education, health, creation of jobs. Even worse, some Western pundits introduced the prejudicial ordering of the concepts of rights: the first generation (civil and political), followed by second generation (social, economic and cultural) and third generation (peace, development, solidarity, and other collective rights). The "Western" approach to human rights was to prioritize the right to property and the right to freedom of expression over the rights to food, water, shelter, and health.

Soon governments discovered that they could instrumentalize human rights to advance geopolitical goals. The Commission on Human Rights was transformed into a gladiator arena in which governments threw daggers and insulted each other instead of trying to cooperate in good faith in order to solve global problems. The practice of "naming and shaming" became ubiquitous; country mandates addressing the situation in specific countries were created to target particular states. In so doing the Commission used double standards, because some of the worst violators of human rights never became targets of "international fact-finding commissions." Meanwhile, the weaponization of human rights was expanded to incorporate many purportedly independent non-governmental organizations, which in fact were well financed by governments and corporations with a view to denouncing and destabilizing geopolitical rivals. In 2006 the Commission was replaced by the Human Rights Council, without, however, returning to the commitment to objectivity and international solidarity originally promoted by P. C. Chang. The hijacking of human rights became even more visible in 2021 when the European Centre for Law and Justice published a well-documented study on the openly political financing of UN Special Rapporteurs, an endemic problem that puts into question their objectivity and independence.

We must celebrate December 10, 2021 in recognition of the spirit of the drafters of the Universal Declaration, and to recall that the UDHR was the common achievement of all nations and peoples, based on all philosophies and religions—from Confucius to Lao-Tse, Buddha, Moses, Aristotle, Jesus Christ, Muhammad, etc. As sisters and brothers who share this common planet Earth, let us rediscover the spirituality of the Universal

Declaration of Human Rights and honor the contribution of P.C. Chang to the development of a universal consciousness of human dignity. Indeed, human rights are not the exclusive domain of any region of the world—they are the common heritage of mankind.

29.

Sapere aude! Dare to Build an Opinion and Defend It

Anyone who has followed the political culture in the U.S., Canada, UK, EU over the past twenty years must have realized that a war on epistemology, on truth, on semantics is going on. We witness the hijacking of concepts like democracy, freedom, peace, patriotism, human rights—and their instrumentalization for domestic and geopolitical purposes. We observe a process of language destruction not unlike what Orwell foresaw in his sadly visionary book *1984.* "Newspeak" is not the future, it is now, *hic et nunc.* We recognize it in the jargon of political correctness, the language and practice of the "cancel culture."

The military-industrial-financial complex in the U.S., Canada, UK, EU is hell bent on full spectrum cognitive control and inundates the population with plausible "narratives" based on fake news, fake history, fake law, fake diplomacy, and fake democracy. We are literally swimming in an ocean of lies—but, remarkably, most people are not conscious of the fact that they are systematically manipulated by governments, corporate media, compliant think tanks and universities. The power of "political correctness" surrounds us in direct and subliminal ways. Most accept it as the "new normal," as long as they continue having access to Hollywood entertainment and lots of sports on television. The classical *panem et circensis* (Juvenal).

A particularly worrisome phenomenon is the gradual emergence of a "human rights industry" that systematically subverts and weaponizes human rights. The holistic approach to civil, political, economic, social and cultural rights advocated by Eleanor Roosevelt has been quietly denatured, dismantled, discarded. We see how the "industry" transforms the individual and collective entitlement to assistance, protection, respect and solidarity—based on our common human dignity—into a hostile arsenal to target competitors and political adversaries.

In the stockpile of *weaponized human rights*, the technique of "naming and shaming" has been accepted—almost become the norm. Yet, experience shows that naming and shaming fails to alleviate the suffering of victims and only satisfies the strategic and propaganda aims of certain governments, non-governmental organizations and of a burgeoning clique of human rights operatives in government, academia and even in international organizations. Allegations of real and putative human rights violations have proven politically very useful to destabilize rival states, denouncing and demonizing them as well as their political leaders. To this end the deliberate use of double-standards, the maximization of human rights violations by a targeted country and the negation or suppression of evidence of violations by our own governments or by our allies, prepares the population to accept patently unjust and illegal actions to unleash "regime change" elsewhere. Precisely this kind of indoctrination of the population through evidence-free allegations and hyperbole paves the way to such barbarism as the aggression against Iraq in 2003 and against Libya in 2011, to name only two emblematic examples.

The Iraq invasion, which UN Secretary General Kofi Annan repeatedly called an "illegal war," nonetheless was supported by a "coalition of the willing"—43 States that turned their backs on the UN Charter and on international law, with the support of many university pundits and the corporate media. One could affirm without fear of contradiction that the Iraq war constituted an international revolt, an assault on the international order established under the UN Charter and a negation of the Nuremberg Principles.

The Iraq war was preceded by a public relations and disinformation scheme of "naming and shaming," a concerted campaign about the non-existent weapons of mass destruction, about the extraordinary criminality of Saddam Hussein, oblivious to the fact that he had a few years earlier he had been our "S.O.B.," doing the Pentagon's bidding in the U.S. proxy war against Iran. Barely eight years later in 2011, alleged human rights violations were again invoked to denounce Muammar al-Gaddafi for the sole purpose of destabilizing Libya, imposing undemocratic "regime change" and facilitating the looting of Libya's natural resources. This occurred in flagrant violation of the customary international law principle of non-intervention in the internal affairs of sovereign States, also contained in treaties and stipulated in the 1986 Judgment of the International Court of Justice in the *Military and Paramilitary Activities in and against Nicaragua* case.[121]

Many rapporteurs of the UN Human Rights Council, European Commission and Inter-American commission also make use of "naming and shaming," a strategy that rests on the false premise that the "namer" somehow possesses moral authority and that the "named" and the global public will recognize this moral superiority and act accordingly. Theoretically this could function if the "namer" were to practice "naming and shaming" uniformly, in a non-selective manner. Alas, the technique frequently backfires, because the "namer" has many skeletons in the closet and engages in blatant double-standards. Such intellectual dishonesty usually stiffens the resistance of the "named" party, who will be even less inclined to take any measures to remedy the alleged violations.

Another technique of norm-warfare is termed "lawfare," whereby the apparatus of the administration of justice, both civil and criminal, is made complicit in the subversion of the rule of law. We witness how domestic and international criminal law are instrumentalized to demonize certain persons and not others. A self-respecting judge would not betray the profession by playing

---

121 International Court of Justice, Military and Paramilitary Activities in and against Nicaragua (Nicaragua v. United States of America), https://www.icj-cij.org/en/case/70/judgments.

this kind of game—but some do—as we have seen by the judges in the U.S., UK, Sweden and Ecuador in the Julian Assange case. Authored by UN Rapporteur on Torture Professor Nils Melzer (Switzerland), originally published in German and now being released in English translation (by the author himself), *The Trial of Julian Assange*[122] reveals the breakdown of the rule of law in the U.S., UK, Sweden and Ecuador—a tour de force, far more serious than Emile Zola's *J'accuse* in 1898 during the *Dreyfus Affaire* in France. Instead of safeguarding the ethos of the rule of law, these political judges corrupt it and should be regarded as of the same ilk as Roland Freisler in relation to Hitler's infamous *Volksgerichtshof!*, thus undermining the credibility of the entire system.

Who will guard over the guardians? *Quis custodiet ipsos custodes* (Juvenal). This is a recurring question of constitutional law. The corruption of the rule of law by those courts that facilitate "lawfare" is far more serious than many will admit, because it is precisely the administration of justice that must be the gatekeeper of truth and equity, the defender of the weak and most vulnerable. The deliberate corruption of the administration of justice to target political or economic rivals leaves us powerless against tyranny.

Under certain conditions, "naming and shaming" as we know it from the practice of politicians, rapporteurs and the media, raises issues of additional violations of human rights and the rule of law, contravening Articles 6, 7, 9, 10, 14, 17, 18, 19 and 26 of the International Covenant on Civil and Political Rights and could reach the threshold of what is termed "hate speech" under Article 20 ICCPR.

Furthermore, despite its propaganda value, experience shows that "naming and shaming" is an ineffective instrument of change of behavior of those accused. States and NGOs would do well to revisit Matthew VII, 3–5, and replace the obsolete

---

122 Verso, New York 2022 [https://www.transcend.org/tms/2021/11/the-trial-of-julian-assange-a-book-by-nils-melzer/].

"naming and shaming" technique by good faith proposals and constructive recommendations, accompanied by the offer of advisory services and technical assistance so as to concretely help whatever actual victims on the ground. Sowing honesty and friendship is necessary if we expect to reap cooperation and progress in human rights terms. What is most needed today is mature diplomacy, results-oriented negotiations, and a culture of dialogue and mediation instead of a petulant culture of posturing, grandstanding, intransigence and holier-than-thou pretence.

The arsenal of weaponized human rights also includes non-conventional conduct of wars such as economic wars and sanctions regimes, ostensibly justified because of the alleged human rights violations of the targeted State. The result is that, far from helping the victims, entire populations are held hostage—now victims not only of violations by their own governments, but also of the "collective punishment" meted out by the sanctioning State(s). This can reach the level of crimes against humanity under article 7 of the Statute of the International Criminal Court, when as a consequence food security is impacted, medicines and medical equipment are rendered scarce or are available only at exorbitant prices. Demonstrably, economic sanctions kill.[123]

It is particularly disgraceful that several non-governmental organizations including Amnesty International and Human Rights Watch have preferred to focus on real and alleged violations of civil and political rights by Venezuela's Nicolas Maduro while forgetting the fundamental human rights of the Venezuelan people as a whole and ignoring the fact that tens of thousands of Venezuelans have already perished as a direct result of illegal unilateral coercive measures and financial blockades, as we know from independent reports, including the 2019 report "Collective Punishment" by Professor Jeffrey Sachs of Columbia University and Mark Weisbrot, of the Center for Economic and Policy Research.[124]

---

123 https://undocs.org/A/HRC/39/47/Add.1
124 Mark Weisbrot and Jeffrey Sachs, "Economic Sanctions as Collective

Another grotesque example of the weaponization of human rights principles is reflected in UN Security Council Resolution 1973 concerning humanitarian assistance to the Libyan population. This resolution was promptly hijacked by NATO to wage an all-out war on Libya, leading to the assassination of Libya's head of State, Muammar Gaddafi, in 2011. Ten years later the country is still mired in civil war and chaos, but the natural resources are safely in the hands of Western economic interests.

Subsequently, in February 2019, USAID and the National Endowment for Democracy organized "humanitarian assistance" for Venezuela and placed an impostor with no constitutional legitimacy, the pretender Juan Guaidó, as the leader who would bring this humanitarian assistance to Venezuela. The operation failed. This was followed by a real coup d'état attempt in April 2019, which again failed, and yet another attempt in May 2020, the *Operation Gideon*, which similarly failed. The violations by the U.S. and accomplices of fundamental norms of international law—and common decency—were breathtaking. And yet, *The New York Times*, *Washington Post*, CNN, Fox, etc. whitewashed these operations and sided with the putschists—invoking "principles" such as "democracy," "humanitarian intervention" and "responsibility to protect." Hypocrisy has indeed come a long way. The non-entity Juan Guaidó is recognized as the Venezuelan President by a certain number of countries to this day!

Yet another form of weaponizing values is the grotesque undermining of peace and human rights by Committees that award prizes in this regard. A notorious disgrace is the undermining of the last will and testament of Alfred Nobel, who genuinely wanted to promote peace and cooperation on global disarmament. If one regards the laureates over the past years, we realize that most of them do not come within the testamentary purpose. Few laureates have been genuine pacifists like Henri Dunant or Bertha von Suttner. They are chosen for purely

Punishment: The Case of Venezuela," April 25, 2019, https://cepr.net/report/economic-sanctions-as-collective-punishment-the-case-of-venezuela/

political purposes—not to advance a demilitarized world order, but to denounce certain governments (in 2021 the Philippines and Russia) and to promote one geopolitical model over another. This is totally against the letter and spirit of the Nobel Peace Prize. The best book on the subject is by Norwegian lawyer Fredrik Heffermehl, *The Nobel Peace Prize: What Nobel really wanted.*[125]

And let us not forget the politicization and weaponization of sports. We are being manipulated into thinking that boycotting the Beijing Olympics is a good and honorable thing. It is not. It is an oxymoron, a public relations stunt.

What can we average citizens do? First and foremost, we must know the facts. And because the corporate media lies to us, we must pro-actively seek out the information. Thanks to the internet, it is still possible to access information that we do not get in *The New York Times* ("all the news that's fit to print"), *Washington Post*, CNN and Fox. We must demand transparency and accountability from our democratically elected leaders, when they engage in confrontational politics instead of formulating constructive solutions to problems. We must demand that our elected officials learn the habits of collaboration and compromise, enable true competition by guaranteeing a level playing field for everyone, both domestically and internationally. Our politicians, the media and the university pundits should embrace a new paradigm: *competition in solidarity.* I incorporate these thoughts into my *25 Principles of International Order,* presented to the UN Human Rights Council in 2018.[126]

---

125 https://www.amazon.com/Nobel-Peace-Prize-Really-Wanted/dp/0313387443; "Stories written by Fredrik S. Heffermehl," *Inter Press Service,* https://www.ipsnews.net/author/fredrik-s-heffermehl/; Fredrik Heffermehl, "Fredrik Heffermehl: The 2021 Nobel Peace Prize: Freedom for the Press or for the U.S.?," *The Transnational,* December 9, 2021, https://transnational.live/2021/12/09/fredrik-heffermehl-the-2021-nobel-peace-prize-freedom-for-the-press-or-for-the-us/.

126 Independent Expert on internatioinal order, "Country Visits," United Nations Human Rights, Office of the High Commissioner, https://www.ohchr.org/en/special-procedures/ie-international-order/country-visits.

Here some practical Resolutions:

1. *Sapere aude* (Horace). Get the facts and act thereon.

2. Push back against the hybrid wars being waged by governments and the media. Demand truth from the government and the private sector. Only on the basis of correct information can the citizens exercise their democratic rights.

3. Push back against the war being waged against whistle-blowers, true human rights defenders. Demand the immediate release of Julian Assange. Recognize the contribution of Edward Snowden to the survival of true American values.

4. Push back against Orwellian newspeak and "political correctness." Refuse to retreat into self-censorship.

5. Push back against the military-industrial-financial complex

In the years to come, let us commit to listen more to others, practice self-criticism and intellectual honesty, stop instrumentalizing values for short-term political gain. Let us reject the weaponization of everything.

30.

A Global Compact on Education

We need education for Peace and International Solidarity. *Pax optima rerum* (peace is the highest good) sums up the recognition of the peace makers at Münster and Osnabrück when they signed the Peace of Westphalia in 1648, ending the mass slaughter of the Thirty Years War. Yet, humanity did not learn the lesson and succeeding generations had to endure the slaughters of the Ottoman wars, the Napoleonic wars, the African wars. Education for peace and international solidarity had never been tried.

Again, one would have expected that after the cataclysm of the Second World War, the Holocaust and the nuclear destruction of Hiroshima and Nagasaki, the world would have learned. Full of hope and determination, delegates at the 1945 San Francisco Conference devised a new world constitution, the UN Charter, followed by the adoption of an International Bill of Rights, concretizing humanity's agreement to live together.

Hundreds of wars since 1945 have taught us that the lessons we thought we had learned were all too soon unlearned. Is it because of lack of a concerted effort to educate younger generations for peace and empathy? Is it because we have the wrong role models and often associate honor and glory with military virtues? Is it because many still think that *dulce et decorum est pro patria mori* (Horace—it is sweet and proper to die for one's country). Should it not be obvious to everybody that what really counts is to live for our countries, to build rather than to destroy?

The purposes and principles of the United Nations place peace, development and human rights at the center of its activities—goals, however, that are not self-executing. Concrete measures must be adopted domestically and internationally to achieve them. Since the 1960s the United Nations has adopted the Convention on the Elimination of Racial Discrimination, the Convention on the Elimination of Discrimination against Women, the Covenant on Civil and Political Rights, the Covenant on Economic, Social and Cultural Rights—all of which emphasize the importance of education to live together. We must continue building on these treaties with patience and perseverance. In this spirit the United Nations adopted the millennium development goals in 2000, and the sustainable development goals in 2015. Goal Nr. 4 of the SDGs commits States to "ensure inclusive and equitable quality education and promote lifelong learning opportunities for all."[127] Civil society has been following-up on these international commitments. For instance, in January 2021 the World Social Forum held a panel on education for peace, sponsored by the International Peace Bureau.[128]

UNESCO and the Office of the UN High Commissioner for Human Rights have done good work in fighting discrimination and the aggressive "animus" that plagues many societies. Although progress has been made, prejudices die hard. In this sense we know that education can be employed for good and bad purposes. In the Rodgers and Hammerstein musical *South Pacific*, Lieutenant Cable sings a bitter song about it:

> You've got to be taught
> to hate and fear
> You've got to be taught
> from year to year,
> It's got to be drummed in your dear little ear
> You've got to be carefully taught.
> You've got to be taught to be afraid
> Of peoples whose eyes are oddly made,

---

127 Goal 4: "Ensure inclusive and equitable quality education and promote lifelong learning opportunities for all," UN Department of Economic and Social Affairs, Sustainable Development, https://sdgs.un.org/goals/goal4.

128 "World Social Forum 2021 Peace Day," International Peace Bureau, https://www.ipb.org/activities/world-social-forum-2021-peace-day/.

And people whose skin is a different shade,
You've got to be carefully taught.
You've got to be taught before it's too late
before you are six or seven or eight,
To hate all the people your relatives hate,
You've got to be carefully taught.

I saw the movie back in 1958, starring the late John Kerr (Cable) and the wonderful Mitzi Gaynor (still alive at 91!). No one who has heard the music or the lyrics ever forgets them.

World religions also teach us that we should strive for peace, and yet religious institutions get instrumentalized precisely to do the opposite, to fight the "infidel," to demand conversion or death. A recent positive development is the launching of the Global Compact on Education[129] in Rome, which goes back to a 2019 initiative by Pope Francis.[130] The idea is the tangible translation of a vision repeatedly spelled out in the apostolic exhortation *Evangelii Gaudium* and further articulated in the encyclical letter *Laudato Sì*. As Pope Francis wrote:

We sense the challenge of finding and sharing a "mystique" of living together, of mingling and encounter, of embracing and supporting one another, of stepping into this flood tide which, while chaotic, can become a genuine experience of fraternity, a caravan of solidarity. . . . (EG 87)

We are invited to take care of the fragility of the most vulnerable, to understand the needs of our fellow men and women.

---

129 Robin Gomes, "Vatican meeting of religions on education to peace, fraternity," *Vatican News*, https://www.vaticannews.va/en/vatican-city/news/2021-10/vatican-meeting-compact-education-religions-peace-fraternity.html (accessed May 24, 2022; Global Compact on Education, https://www.educationglobalcompact.org/en/.

130 Global Compact on Education, *Instrumentum Laboris,* https://www.educationglobalcompact.org/resources/Risorse/instrumentum-laboris-en.pdf.

The goal must be to establish a culture of peace based on mutual respect, historical truth and empathy. Achieving this goal, however, requires education from an early age, and re-education of older generations, because we know that we have a long heritage of violence, and our aggressive habits, egoism and greed must be tamed.

In the encyclical letter *Laudato Sì*, we are reminded that "education will be inadequate and ineffectual unless we strive to promote a new way of thinking about human beings, life, society and our relationship with nature" (n. 215).

Everyone—not only children—should be educated in compromise, cooperation, empathy, solidarity, compassion, restoration, mediation and reconciliation. Negotiation skills must be taught so as to prevent breaches of the peace and other forms of violence as well as to ensure a peaceful continuation of life after conflict. A philosophical paradigm change is necessary to break out of the prevailing culture of violence, the logic of power, practices of economic exploitation, cultural imperialism and impunity. A road map to this culture of peace entails a strategy to identify and remove obstacles, among which are the arms race, unilateralism and the tendency to apply international law *à la carte*.

31.

Disarmament for Development

"In the councils of government, we must guard against the acquisition of unwarranted influence, whether sought or unsought, by the military-industrial complex. The potential for the disastrous rise of misplaced power exists and will persist. We must never let the weight of this combination endanger our liberties or democratic processes."
—Dwight D. Eisenhower, January 17, 1961[131]

Our governments have the wrong priorities. Their budgetary priorities are totally skewed. Year after year Americans' tax dollars are being squandered by Congress, which adopts military-first budgets instead of human-security budgets. As I documented in my 2014 report to the UN Human Rights Council,[132] and as we know from published documents, some 40% of our budget goes to the military—ultimately, trillions of dollars for war, military interventions, military propaganda, missiles, drones, military bases at home and abroad, military exercises, and who knows what else? We know that billions are unaccounted for. Where have all the missing billions gone?

If we were a truly democratic country, we would be asked whether we would like to prioritize war or education, whether we would like to give the priority to disarmament and peace negotiations rather than to pursue an arms race, whether we want weapons to be sent to warring countries, or whether we would prefer to be an honest broker and mediate for peace.

---

131 "Military-Industrial Complex Speech, Dwight D. Eisenhower, 1961," The Avalon Project, Yale Law School, https://avalon.law.yale.edu/20th_century/eisenhower001.asp.
132 A/HRC/27/51.

We should be able to vote on specific aspects of our national budget. We would not rely on our system of so-called "representative democracy," which in reality does *not* represent us, to make our views carry weight. The reality is that we have a "dysfunctional" democracy, which mostly allows us only to vote for candidate A or candidate B, both of whom are subsidized by and committed to the military-industrial complex, both of whom want huge military budgets, both of whom prefer sabre-rattling and military adventures over dialogue, tension over détente, predator competition over international cooperation.

In a world threatened by pandemics, climate change, earthquakes, tsunamis and other natural disasters, it is time to practice international solidarity with the rest of humanity to solve global problems. Our governments should begin by respecting the sovereignty of other states, refrain from interfering in their international affairs as stipulated in General Assembly Resolutions 2131, 2625, 3314. They must stop provocations, silence the drums of war, stop the enormously costly arms race and observe article 2(3) of the UN Charter, which commits all member states to solve their differences by negotiation, peaceful means, and in good faith.

Although most politicians in East and West, North and South give lip service to the importance of local, regional and international peace, they actually undermine peace on a daily basis. Although they are ostensibly committed to achieving the 17 Sustainable Development Goals by 2030, there is no reasonable prospect whatever of achieving them, since military budgets are expanding, not contracting, and the propaganda for war has grown exponentially. Wherever we look in the media—the "quality press," Hollywood, televised news, internet news, the social media—everyone seems to be engaging in or paying lip service to fake news, skewed narratives, and giving full faith and credit to false flag operations. The recklessness of such behavior might eventually lead to an error of judgment by a senior politician a computer glitch, a fateful human error or to an irrepressible public bellicosity overwhelming political leaders' more prudent options—that will result in a nuclear confrontation with Russia, China or other nuclear powers.

Instead of cutting military budgets to help combat Covid-19 and other pandemics, we observe the recklessness of governments that privatized hospitals and closed clinics, because they were not generating sufficient revenue. The right to health is a human right and governments are ontologically obliged to take appropriate measures to advance the health of the population. What we have seen over the past decades is neglect, and unpreparedness. That is the reason why the United States has suffered over one million deaths from Covid-19.

Our response to the pandemic reveals the downward spiral of research for preparedness to tackle emergencies. In the first two decades of the 21st century many countries reduced their investment in health, education, social services, infrastructure while wasting taxpayers' money in the development and procurement of fighter jets and lethal autonomous weapon systems. Lobbies for the military-industrial complex are fuelling wars worldwide, because they can only make a profit if the weapons are used and destroyed, thus triggering the necessity to replace them. Thus. the vicious circle continues. Produce weapons, increase tensions, provoke armed conflict, blow up the weapons in real war, produce new weapons, make a profit.

Article 2, paragraph 4, of the UN Charter stipulates that States shall refrain not only from the actual use of force in international relations, but also from the *threat* of the use of force. This international law principle is concretized in article 20 of the International Covenant on Civil and Political Rights, which specifically prohibits propaganda for war. Article 20, paragraph 2, specifically prohibits incitement to hatred and violence. How else can we describe the Russophobia and Sinophobia exhibited by many of our politicians? How often is this international law principle cited by way of rebuke?

Notwithstanding these norms, many "leaders" and political "pundits" in the U.S. and NATO countries engage in inflammatory provocations and "military exercises" next to the borders of States, where we would like to see "regime change." What is particularly dangerous is that these provocations are applauded and magnified by political commentators and the mainstream media which really should know better.

CODIFYING PEACE AS A HUMAN RIGHT

Based on the UN Charter's call to save succeeding generations from the scourge of war, civil society is leading the movement to codify peace as a human right with clearly defined individual and collective dimensions. This initiative was enshrined in the *Santiago Declaration* of December 10, 2010, which led to a draft declaration on the right to peace by the Advisory Committee of the UN Human Rights Council, a document manifesting a holistic approach to peace and encompassing, civil, cultural, economic, political and social rights. In my capacity as UN Independent Expert on International Order, I participated in all of the consultations of the inter-governmental working group on the right to peace. It was a painful and revealing experience. Anyone who desires to know which countries are truly for human dignity and human rights and which countries are against, should have been an observer at these disgraceful meetings, in which representatives of the Unites States and NATO countries outright denied that there was anything like a human right to peace. Worse still, they argued that there *should not be* such a right. Their arguments were not only wrong on the law—they were morally reprehensible.

The watered-down resolution eventually adopted by the General Assembly[133] on December 19, 2016 is, however, not the end of the story. Civil society is not about to give up, and the Spanish Society for International Human Rights Law, which

---

133 https:/undocs.org/en/A/RES/71/189

spearheaded the *Declaración de Santiago*, continues its educational work to convince a majority of states of the urgency to recognize peace as a principal human right. States must listen to civil society and complete the work already stated by the General Assembly in its Resolution 39/11 of November 12, 1984, adopted at the height of the cold war.[134] The renewed cold war and the hot war in Ukraine suggest that the General Assembly must revisit the issue all the more urgently and adopt a new resolution affirming all the constitutive elements of the right to peace.

What is most necessary today is for States to work collaboratively together on resolving the root causes of local, regional and international conflict, often emerging from the unrepresentative nature of governments, the huge disconnect between power and people, the great injustices and inequalities prevailing in the world, the race for natural resources, the asymmetries of trade relations, the imposition of illegal sanctions and financial blockades on other States, and the criminal manipulation of public opinion by governments and media.

Over the past seventy years many armed conflicts and several genocidal wars had their origin in the denial of the right of internal or external self-determination. There are still many indigenous peoples, non-self-governing peoples, peoples living under occupation, peoples who have suffered gross violations of their human rights, who have a legitimate claim to self-determination—including the Palestinians, the Tamils of Sri Lanka, the Sahraouis, the Mapuches, the West Papuans, the Catalans, the Corsicans, the Armenians of Nagorno Karabakh, the Southern Tyrolians, and, yes, also the much maligned peoples of Abkhazia, Southern Ossetia, Crimea, Donetsk and Lugansk. It is high time for the United Nations to proactively promote the realization of

---

134 "Declaration on the Right of Peoples to Peace," UN General Assembly resolution 39/11 adopted November 12, 1984, United Nations Human Rights, Office of the High Commissioner, https:/www.ohchr.org/EN/Professionalinterest/Pages/ RightOfPeoplesToPeace.aspx.

self-determination as a conflict-prevention strategy, requiring mediation and, where appropriate, United Nations organized and monitored referenda. It is not the right of self-determination that causes conflict, but the unjust denial thereof. Countless wars since the WWII have been triggered precisely by the intransigence of politicians, by their lack of flexibility, by their insistence on the obsolete principle of *uti possidetis*.

Addressing global problems including the challenges of the Sustainable Development Goals requires trillions of dollars. It is therefore imperative to drastically reduce military expenditures and convert war economies into peace economies, and thereby create millions of jobs in the education, health and social sectors. It is unconscionable to continue the arms race, when millions of human beings worldwide are suffering from extreme poverty, famine and no access to clean water and sanitation.

Nuclear states must also engage in good faith disarmament negotiations as required by article 6 of the Non-Proliferation Treaty. The threat of nuclear annihilation will persist for as long as the production and stockpiling of nuclear weapons is not eliminated. This concern has been the subject of two General Comments adopted by the UN Human Rights Committee on article 6 of the International Covenant on Civil and Political Rights, the right to life. It should be clear to everybody that without peace, we cannot exercise our human rights. Let us conclude with a warning by President Eisenhower: "Every gun that is made, every warship launched, every rocket fired signifies, in the final sense, a theft from those who hunger and are not fed, those who are cold and are not clothed."[135]

Disarmament for Development must be our mantra.

---

135 Dwight D. Eisenhower, "The Chance for Peace," transcript of speech given April 16, 1953 to an association of American newspaper editors in Washington, D.C., Social Justice Speeches, *SoJust* http://www.edchange.org/multicultural/speeches/ ike_chance_for_peace.html

32.

A New Health Order for the World[136]

136 On May 22, 2020 I published my first of several articles on a post-COVID social contract, in the journal of the Geneva-based international association South-Centre, *Southviews,* No. 197. [See https://dezayasalfred.wordpress.com/2020/05/25/south-centre-the-post-covid-world-needs-a-new-social-contract/.] One of my doctoral students at the Geneva School of Diplomacy was and still is employed with WHO and she made my essays available to Secretary-General Dr. Tedros Adhanom Ghebreyesus. At the June 2021 GSD graduation ceremony I had the opportunity of personally discussing some of my initiatives with Dr. Ghebreyesus. It seems that some of them were taken seriously, since in December the World Health Assembly decided to start working on a global pandemic prevention treaty [World Health Organization, "World Health Assembly agrees to launch process to develop historic global accord on pandemic prevention, preparedness and response," December 1, 2021, https://www.who.int/news/item/01-12-2021-world-health-assembly-agrees-to-launch-process-to-develop-historic-global-accord-on-pandemic-prevention-preparedness-and-response]. During the 75th WHO World Health Assembly held May 22–28, 2022 in Geneva, the implications of such a treaty were discussed. [See WHO, *A Potential Framework Convention for Pandemic Preparedness and Response,* Member States Briefing, March 18, 2021, https://apps.who.int/gb/COVID-19/pdf_files/2021/18_03/Item2.pdf; World Economic Forum, "Do we need an international treaty for future crises? These 23 leaders think so," Reuters, March 30, 2021, https://www.weforum.org/agenda/2021/03/new-treaty-aims-to-unite-nations-in-preparation-for-future-pandemics/; and "What is the proposed WHO Pandemic Preparedness Treaty?" *House of Commons Library,* May 18, 2022, https://commonslibrary.parliament.uk/research-briefings/cbp-9550/.] However, there was also a certain backlash. [See Adam Taylor, "Why the WHO is pushing for a global 'pandemic treaty,'" *The Washington Post,* November 11, 2021, https://www.washingtonpost.com/world/2021/11/11/who-global-pandemic-treaty/, and "African Nations Force WHO to Back Down on Pandemic Treaty," *SEEMOREROCKS,* June 1, 2022, https://seemorerocks.is/african-nations-force-who-to-back-down-on-pandemic-treaty/.] See earlier articles: World Health Organization, "Global leaders unite in urgent call for international pandemic treaty," March 30, 2021, https://www.who.int/news/item/30-03-2021-global-leaders-unite-in-urgent-call-for-international-pandemic-treaty, and World Health Assembly (About), https://www.who.int/about/governance/world-health-assembly. See also European Parliament, Parliamentary question on WHO pandemic treaty, March 7, 2022, https://www. europarl.europa.eu/doceo/document/P-9-2022-000921_EN.html.

Many political scientists, economists, lawyers, historians, journalists and civil society activists have come to realize that the post-Covid world should not merely "pick up where we left off," but actually requires a new social contract, one that will have better budgetary priorities, place people over profits, adopt concrete measures to advance equality and social justice. International solidarity and emergency preparedness must be strengthened to jointly face global challenges. Resuming "business as usual" is not an option. The health crisis we are suffering and the pathetic mismanagement by many countries is the direct result of failed neo-liberal policies that must be revisited and corrected if the planet is going to survive.

What should the new priorities be? Surely the role of the World Health Organization must be strengthened and expanded, with its donor base coming from governments rather than from independent billionaires who have skin in the game, and with an independent and international science advisory board and supporting institutions, for the same purpose of establishing policies not burdened by conflicts of interest. The International Health Regulations must be reassessed, and a revised treaty should be adopted with provisions for faster and more effective international cooperation. The focus must be on prevention of disease and contagion, early warning and facilitation of exchange of information. Not only the WHO but all national and regional health authorities must devote time and resources to finding cures to current and future viruses, HIV/AIDS, cancer, heart disease, emphysema, Alzheimer's, Parkinson's, multiple sclerosis, malaria, tuberculosis. We have a moral obligation to endeavor to eradicate all diseases and not only those with potential of international spread. We need much more than just "band aids" and palliatives to alleviate current pain. We need properly funded institutions—industry independent health "think tanks"—to anticipate future crises. As the world population, particularly in Europe, Japan, China, and Australia becomes older, we owe it to our parents and grandparents to address all the issues that come with aging. The planet is rich and bountiful—and older people should not be discarded by society but should enjoy the last years of earthly life in dignity.

It is in this sense that the United Nations Secretary-General should convene a World Conference on Pandemic Preparedness with the task of elaborating a Plan of Action, a world agenda based on multilateralism and coordination by all UN and regional agencies, with broad participation by inter-governmental organizations, like IOM and South Centre, the International Committee of the Red Cross, non-governmental organizations, universities and civil society. Now is the time for António Guterres to confer with advisors from all disciplines and all regions, including economists Jeffrey Sachs, Joseph Stiglitz and Thomas Piketty, and make concrete proposals to world leaders on how best to elevate health standards worldwide and how best to strengthen world peace by reforming the financial institutions, world trade and disaster relief in conformity with the Purposes and Principles of the UN Charter, taking due account of General Assembly Resolutions 2625 and 3314.

The COVID-19 pandemic can be a game-changer, a historic opportunity to radically rethink the prevailing financial and economic system characterized by its boom-and-bust cycles, widespread unemployment, and demonstrably unjust distribution of wealth, which have left societies inadequately prepared to deal with crises including pandemics, hurricanes, earthquakes, tsunamis, volcanic eruptions and, of course, the consequences of global warming.[137]

---

137 United Nations, "'We Are Only as Strong as the Weakest', Secretary-General Stresses, at Launch of Economic Report on COVID-19 Pandemic," March 31, 2020, https://www.un.org/press/en/2020/sgsm20029.doc.htm; CGTN, "UN chief says mankind 'so unprepared' for COVID-19, world lacks solidarity," May 15, 2020; https://news.cgtn.com/news/2020-05-15/ UN-chief-says-mankind-so-unprepared-for-COVID-19-Qvi8tVla2k/index. html; "The Secretary-General's UN COVID-19 Response and Recovery Fund (April 2020)," *OHCA reliefweb*, May 4, 2020, https://reliefweb.int/report/ world/secretary-generals-un-covid-19-response-and-recovery-fund-april-2020;

It would be a great shame if we lose this opportunity to take our future in our hands, and if we allow the World-Economic Forum to push through its neo-liberal scam called *The Great Reset Initiative*.[138] We must say "no" to the WEC and look for solutions in the genuinely progressive and humanistic World Social Forum[139] and its Porto Alegre Manifesto.

A new social contract will require a paradigm shift in the prevailing economic, trade and social models—which already are being upended and require new rules, if the world is to recover unity from trends breaking it into blocs. Governments bear responsibility for their unwise and inequitable budgetary allocations, which prioritize military expenditures over investment in health, education and people-centered infrastructures. In the light of the Covid pandemic, every country should immediately reduce military and non-essential expenditures and focus on resolving the problems and complications that accompany the pandemic as a matter of urgency.

This is a propitious moment for the Members of the United Nations to address the inevitably emerging multipolarity due to events related to Ukraine, China and Russia, which appear to be bringing globalization to a screeching halt. This perhaps should not be mourned. While globalization has brought many good things, it has also been accompanied by extreme poverty and endemic social injustice. Going forward, we should seek to reform the outdated Bretton Woods institutions[140] and to reorganize economic and trade priorities so as to achieve the

---

United Nations Secretary-General, "Launch of Global Humanitarian Response Plan for COVID-19," March 25, 2020, https://www.un.org/sg/en/content/sg/press-encounter/2020-03-25/launch-of-global-humanitarian-response-plan-for-covid-19.

138 World Economic Forum, "The Great Reset," https://www.weforum.org/great-reset.

139 World Social Forum, https://www.foranewwsf.org/gb/test/.

140 My 2017 report to the Human Rights Council [https://ap.ohchr.org/documents/dpage_e.aspx?si=A/HRC/36/40] and my 2017 report to the General Assembly [https://www.un.org/en/ga/search/view_doc.asp?symbol=A/72/187] formulate concrete proposals on how to reform the World Bank and the International Monetary Fund so that they are no longer "human rights free zones."

Sustainable Development Goals (SDGs) and give practical meaning to the right of self-determination of all peoples and their right to development.

In this context, a World Conference on Pandemic Preparedness, with a mandate to revive multilateralism and pursue multipolar engagement, must ensure the proper funding of all UN agencies and establish mechanisms to enhance their coordination and efficiency. But the conference, if it is going to have added value, must go beyond cosmetic adjustments and a perfunctory return to the broken *status quo ante*. The Conference must promote all-hazard emergency preparedness, also with regard to coordinated policies to address emerging global dangers, such as potential asteroid impacts. And it must have legal import. It must be equipped with an "observatory," a monitoring and enforcement mechanism. Otherwise the conference would only be—well, just another conference.

For now it is not a question of making specific amendments to the UN Charter under Article 108, but the Conference should issue a pledge, a good faith statement reaffirming the universality of the Purposes and Principles of the United Nations as the best hope of humanity, and committing to applying the UN Charter as a kind of world constitution,[141] respecting the judgments and advisory opinions of the International Court of Justice as the authoritative statements of a world constitutional court. This would entail the progressive incorporation of UN Charter provisions into the domestic legislation of UN Member States.

A world conference could revisit the Four Freedoms of Franklin Delano Roosevelt, rediscover the spirituality of the Universal Declaration of Human Rights, revive the legacy of Eleanor Roosevelt, René Cassin, Charles Malik, P.C. Chang and John Humphrey. The paradigm shift entails a change in national

---

141 See my 25 Principles of International Order published as Chapter 2 in my book, *Building a Just World Order* (Atlanta, Ga.: Clarity Press, 2021), and the earlier 23 principles formulated in my 2018 report to the Human Rights Council, paragraph 14.

budgetary priorities, away from the arms race, war, military bases, procurement, drones and missiles. What is urgent and feasible is a gradual, step by step conversion of military-first budgets into human-security budgets.

Indeed, a significant reduction in military expenditures could liberate necessary funds to actually achieve the UN's SDGs and advance the enjoyment of all human rights by all, including and most importantly the right to health, food, water, shelter, etc. Taxpayers' money that has been wasted in Orwellian "mass surveillance" activities, such as those revealed by Edward Snowden,[142] must be redirected to social services. In my 2014 report to the UN Human Rights Council I recommended that the military establishment be gradually converted into peacetime industries at all levels, creating many more jobs in education, healthcare, housing, environmental protection and other social services.[143]

A World Conference on Pandemic Preparedness should call for states to take measures to abolish tax havens and ensure the payment of taxes by investors and transnational corporations without phony registrations or "sweetheart deals."[144] The failures of the neoliberal ideology, the systematic exploitation of peoples worldwide, the destruction of the environment and the constant threat posed by the arms race, stockpiling of weapons of mass destruction, research & development programs into lethal autonomous weapon systems and other aberrations have become

---

142 Edward Snowden, *Permanent Record* (New York: Metropolitan Books, 2019).

143 Alfred de Zayas, "Report of the Independent Expert on the promotion of a democratic and equitable international order," United Nations Human Rights, Office of the High Commissioner, https://ap.ohchr.org/documents/dpage_e.aspx?si=A/HRC/27/51. A consultation convened by me in Brussels in May 2014 indicated how little academics and think tanks have been thinking about this necessary conversion. The best information came from Colin Archer of the International Peace Bureau [http://www.ipb.org/].

144 My 2016 report to the General Assembly was devoted specifically to the criminalization of tax fraud and tax evasion, is available at https://ap.ohchr.org/documents/dpage_e.aspx?si=A/71/286.

all too evident. Surely the gravity of the COVID-19 pandemic would have been considerably less lethal if governments had implemented human-rights centred economies in which the right to life and the right to health had enjoyed priority over market speculation, the drive to make short-term profits, and the senseless exploitation of the planet to the point of ecocide that today threatens the well-being of billions of human beings. This would have been more possible, were it not for IMF conditionalities which prioritize indebted countries' export development and debt repayment while restricting their social spending. Targeting changes in IMF rules could impact the wellbeing of a range of countries.

Civil society in all countries should now demand from their governments a new social contract based on the implementation of the ten core UN human rights treaties. Admittedly, the task of standard-setting has not been completed, since codification of human rights is never definitive and never exhaustive but constitutes an evolutionary *mode d'emploi* for the exercise of civil, cultural, economic, political and social rights.

Alas, the interpretation and application of human rights have been hindered by sterile positivism and a regrettable tendency to focus only on individual rights while forgetting collective rights. It is all too obvious that many in the "human rights industry" show little or no interest for the social responsibilities that accompany the exercise of rights and fail to see the necessary symbiosis of rights and obligations as formulated in Article 29 of the Universal Declaration of Human Rights.

A new post-Covid social contract should follow the motto of the International Labour Organisation—*si vis pacem, cole justitiam*—in order to achieve peace, it is necessary to cultivate justice. Thus, a post-Covid conference should revisit the UN Charter and adopt multilateral measures that will strengthen the UN system so that the three pillars of peace, development and human rights are better served. Virginia Dandan in her 2017 report to the Human Rights Council presented a draft declaration on international solidarity.[145] That is precisely what the world needs now. Indeed, our post-Covid priorities must be achieving a democratic and equitable international order based on solidarity which must be responsive to the needs of all members of the human family—not just to the whims of the 1%—or indeed to the formation of politico-economic blocs resulting from the Russia-Ukraine events that led to the unleashing of unprecedented sanctions and concomitant measures to circumvent them.

Given the likelihood of succeeding waves of pandemics, the need for international solidarity remains, and should only foster the recognition of the need to help each other equitably and rationally, to eradicate hunger, to ensure education for peace, to tackle the challenges of climate change and to build a democratic and equitable world order. Another world is indeed possible, but we must all work for it.

---

145 Virginia Dandan, "Draft declaration on the right to international solidarity," United Nations Human Rights, Office of the High Commissioner, https://www.ohchr.org/Documents/Issues/Solidarity/DraftDeclarationRightInternationalSolidarity.pdf

33.

Overhauling the Human Rights Apparatus: A New Paradigm for the 21st Century

Every institution requires periodic reviews in order to take stock of its achievements and failures and develop new strategies for the future. A comprehensive forensic investigation of the vast human rights apparatus domestically and internationally has become necessary. The early diagnosis is not good—the human rights system is in many ways sclerotic and in urgent need of reform, adjustment, recalibration, reorientation. Although the human rights apparatus has enormously grown and expanded since the adoption of the 1948 Universal Declaration of Human Rights (UDHR), although progress has been achieved in the eradication of poverty, extending education to all, and combatting discrimination, there remain chronic problems in the entire system and symptoms of widespread dysfunctionality in the corpus—not only in its machinery but also in its operational psychology. It seems like the spirituality of the UDHR has been lost. Many noble values have simply been hijacked for ulterior purposes, and human rights norms weaponized to destabilize geopolitical rivals.

Politicians, NGOs and UN secretariat members master the jargon of human rights, to which they only give lip service; most of them are only going through the motions and falling into a human rights "routine" that fails to see the faces of the victims. At the UN Human Rights Council, we witness mostly diplomatic rituals, and an effort not to shake the boat too much. Admittedly, there have been successes, which the apparatchiks and a compliant corporate media effusively hail. But they hide the root causes of human rights violations, the economic imbalances and continuing exploitation. They propose the wrong treatment for most ailments, applying band-aids here and there, without developing a coherent preventative plan encompassing, say, early detection of disease, effective curative measures and the rehabilitation of the disabled.

We know that the UN Division of Human Rights evolved into the Centre for Human Rights and then the Office of the High Commissioner for Human Rights (General Assembly Resolution 48/141). As it turned out, the HR directors are more "managers" than committed human rights leaders inspired by a genuine belief in the fraternity of human beings and the equal dignity of all. The UN Secretariat is more politicized than ever, and many have forgotten the sources of the UDHR and the enthusiasm of the creative days of Eleanor Roosevelt, René Cassin, Charles Malik and P.C. Chang.

The much-maligned UN Commission on Human Rights evolved into the Human Rights Council, which is more politicized than its predecessor. In particular, the selection of "independent experts" and "special rapporteurs" must be overhauled, because most rapporteurs simply grandstand, engage in naming and shaming, and forget that there are victims out there who need our help and not only our words. This entails the provision of advisory services and technical assistance—not just pointing fingers from our high horses. Many rapporteurs simple toe the line of the powerful, making them, ultimately, in the service of the status quo.

Any road plan to recovery must recognize that all human rights derive from human dignity. The codification is never definitive and never exhaustive but constitutes an evolutionary *mode d'emploi* for the exercise of civil, cultural, economic, political and social rights. Alas, the interpretation and application of human rights is hindered by wrong priorities, sterile legal positivism and a regrettable tendency to focus only on individual rights while forgetting collective rights. On the other hand, many rights advocates show little or no interest for the social responsibilities that accompany the exercise of rights and fail to see the necessary symbiosis of rights and obligations, notwithstanding the letter and spirit of article 29 of the UDHR.

The time has come to change the human rights paradigm away from narrow positivism toward a broader understanding of human rights norms in the context of an emerging customary international law of human rights. Law is neither physics nor mathematics, but a dynamic human institution that day by day addresses the needs and aspirations of society, adjusting here, filling lacunae there. Every human rights lawyer knows that the spirit of the law (Montesquieu) transcends the limitations of the letter of the law, and hence codified norms should always be interpreted in the light of those general principles of law that inform all legal systems: good faith, proportionality and *ex injuria non oritur jus*.

I propose discarding the obsolete and artificial division of human rights into those of the falsely called first generation (civil and political), second (economic, social and cultural) and third generation (environment, peace, development) rights—with its obvious predisposition to favor civil and political rights. This generational divide is part of a structure that perpetuates a world order that much too often appears to allow injustice.

Instead, I propose a functional paradigm that would consider rights in the light of their function within a coherent system—not of competing rights and aspirations, but of interrelated, mutually reinforcing rights which should be applied in their interdependence and understood in the context of a coordinated strategy to serve the ultimate goal of achieving human dignity in all of its manifestations. These four categories would replace the skewed narrative of three generations of rights.

1. **Enabling rights**, which would include the rights to food, water, shelter, development, homeland, education—but also the right to peace, since one cannot enjoy human rights unless there is an environment conducive to the exercise of those rights. Article 28 of

the UDHR postulates the right of every human being "to a social and international order in which the rights and freedoms set forth in this Declaration can be fully realized." This entails the basic necessities of life and the right to a level playing field.

2. **Immanent or inherent rights**, such as the right to equality, the right to non-arbitrariness. Indeed, every right necessarily contains in itself the element of equality, the self-evident requirement that it be applied equally and equitably, that there be uniformity and pre- dictability (what the Germans call *Rechtssicherheit*). Immanent rights also encompass the rights to life, integrity, liberty and security of person, in the light of which other rights must be interpreted and applied. There are also inherent limitations to the exercise of rights. The general principle of law prohibiting abuse of rights (*sic utere tuo ut alienum non laedas* – use your right without harming others, a principle advocated by Sir Hersh Lauterpacht as an overarching norm prohibiting the egoistic exercise of rights to achieve anti-social results or unjust enrichment) means that every right, also a human right, must be exercised in the context of other rights and not instrumentalized to destroy other rights or harm others. There is no right to intransigence as we know from Shylock in the *Merchant of Venice*. The letter of the law must never be used against the spirit of the law.

3. **Instrumental rights,** a category of procedural rights, such as the rights to due process, access to informa- tion, freedom of expression and peaceful assembly, the right to form labour unions, social security, leisure—rights that we need to achieve our potential, to complete our personalities, to engage in the pursuit of happiness.

4. **End rights or outcome rights**, that is, the concrete exercise of human dignity, that condition of life that allows each human being to be himself or herself. This ultimate right is the *right to our identity*, to our privacy, the right to be ourselves, to think by ourselves and express our humanity without indoctrination, without intimidation, without pressures of political correctness, without having to sell ourselves, without having to engage in self-censorship. The absence of this outcome right to identity and self-respect is reflec- ted in much of the strife we see in the world today. It is through the consciousness and exercise of the right to our identity and the respect of the identity of others that we will enjoy the individual and collective right to peace.[146]

A meeting of the United Nations Human Rights Council, February 2020, Geneva. [GOVERNMENTZA / FLICKR]

---

146   See my 2013 report to the GA A/68/284, paras. 67–68.

The United Nations Human Rights Council should become the international arena where governments compete to show how best to implement human rights, how to strengthen the rule of law, how to achieve social justice, where they display best practices and give life to this new functional paradigm of human rights. This kind of competition in human rights performance is the noblest goal and challenge for civilization. The Council should become the preeminent forum where governments elucidate what they themselves have done and are doing to deliver on human rights, in good-faith implementation of pledges, in adherence to a daily culture of human rights characterized by generous interpretation of human rights treaties and a commitment to the inclusion of all stakeholders.

What the Council must not be is a politicized arena where gladiators use human rights as weapons to defeat their political adversaries and where human rights are undermined through "side shows," the "flavor of the month" or "legal black holes." The civilization model of the globalized world must not be one of positivism, legalisms and loopholes, but one of ethics, direct democracy, respect for the environment, international solidarity and human dignity.

When overhauling the human rights apparatus, we need not only doctors, psychologists, experts in education and propaganda, we also need the legal profession. Unfortunately, many lawyers are "pens for rent" or "intellectual mercenaries." One would think that government lawyers and lawyers employed in the human rights apparatus should be conscious of their special responsibilities to humanity. They should see their role as that of facilitators of enforcement of just laws both nationally and internationally. They should devote their efforts to translating international commitments into concrete action and crafting the necessary measures to comply with treaties and the rules of international judicial and quasi-judicial bodies including the International Court of Justice and the UN Human Rights Committee.

In order to overhaul the human rights apparatus we need lawyers who are committed to making human rights, juridical, justiciable and enforceable. Lawyers, UN Secretariat members, NGOs and civil society can all cooperate in making the promise of the UDHR a reality for all men, women and children in the planet.

IN CLOSING

Let us close this collection of essays with quotations from two great human beings who demonstrated through their actions that they believed in the dignity of the human being and in our responsibility as citizens to actively contribute to the promotion and protection of human rights worldwide.

In his farewell address of January 1981, former U.S. President Jimmy Carter pointed out that:
The battle for human rights, at home and abroad, is far from over. We should never be surprised nor discouraged, because the impact of our efforts has had and will always have varied results. Rather, we should take pride that the ideals which gave birth to our Nation still inspire the hopes of oppressed people around the world. We have no cause for self-righteousness or complacency, but we have every reason to persevere, both within our own country and beyond our borders.

If we are to serve as a beacon for human rights, we must continue to perfect here at home the rights and the values which we espouse around the world: a decent education for our children, adequate medical care for all Americans, an end to discrimination against minorities and women, a job for all those able to work, and freedom from injustice and religious intolerance.[147]

---

147 Jimmy Carter, Farewell Address to the Nation, January 14, 1981, The American Presidency Project, https://www.presidency.ucsb.edu/documents/farewell-address-the-nation-0

Eleanor Roosevelt's 1958 address to the General Assembly made the same appeal:

Where, after all, do universal rights begin? In places close to home, so close and so small that cannot be seen on any maps of the world. Yet they are the world of the individual person; the neighborhood he lives in; the school or college he attends; the factory, farm, or office where he works. Such are the places where every man, woman and child seeks equal justice, equal opportunity, equal dignity without discrimination. Unless these rights have meaning there, they have little meaning anywhere. Without concerted citizen action to uphold them close to home, we shall look in vain for progress in the large world.[148]

---

148 Eleanor Roosevelt, *The Great Question* (New York: United Nations, 1958). Lise Kingo, "The Great Question: Where Do Human Rights Begin for Business?" *Huffpost,* August 18, 2017, https://www.huffpost.com/entry/the-great-question-where-do-human-rights-begin-for_b_59971610e4b033e0fbdec37a. Alfred de Zayas, "Eleanor Roosevelt's legacy—that's how to build back better," UN staff journal *newSpecial,* March 2022, p. 35, https://www.newspecial.org. The San Francisco NGO *Eleanor Lives* is committed to building back better by safeguarding the legacy of Eleanor Roosevelt, https://www.eleanorlives.org. An international conference is being organized for 10 December 2023 to mark the 75th anniversary of the adoption of the Universal Declaration of Human Rights by the UN General Assembly, https://wetheaction.org/projects/879-help-nonprofit-eleanor-lives-draft-an-international-bill-of-rights.

Index